Mastering the Guitar

A COMPREHENSIVE METHOD FOR TODAY'S GUITARIST!

CLASS METHOD
Level 1/Beginning
9th Grade and Higher

By William Bay & Mike Christiansen

Online Audio www.melbay.com/99553EB

CONTENTS

1 2 3 4 5 6 7 8 9 0

D1601856

Visit us on the Web at www.melbay.com — E-mail us at email@melbay.com

Types of Guitars

CLASSIC GUITAR

STANDARD FLATTOP GUITAR

JUMBO FOLK GUITAR

TWELVE-STRING GUITAR

ARCH-TOP

SOLID-BODY ELECTRIC

HOLLOW BODY ELECTRIC

CLASSIC GUITAR – This is an acoustic (non-electric) guitar. The classic guitar is characterized by the round sound hole, nylon or gut strings, and a rather wide neck. The reason for the wide neck is to allow the right-hand fingers to fit in between the strings for fingerstyle playing. The wood on a classic guitar is usually lighter than on a regular folk-style guitar in order to bring out the delicate tone of the nylon strings. Never put metal strings on a guitar made for nylon strings. The wood will not be able to stand the increased stress. We sometimes recommend starting on nylon strings, as they are easier (less painful) on the fingers.

STANDARD FLATTOP GUITAR – This is a very widely used guitar today. It is an acoustic guitar which may be played with the fingers or with a pick. It is characterized by steel strings and a more narrow neck than is found on the "classic"-type guitars. The narrow neck makes it easier to finger barre chords or more complicated chords. This type of guitar puts out considerably more volume than a nylon-stringed or classical guitar. We recommend using light or extra light gauge strings for beginning students

JUMBO FOLK GUITAR – This style of guitar is similar to the standard flattop guitar except for the larger body. While the large body on this type is bulkier to handle, a fuller and deeper tone results from it. Some flattop guitars come with a wide neck to facilitate fingerstyle performance.

TWELVE-STRING GUITAR – The 12-string guitar has a large body which is similar to a jumbo model. The neck is wider in order to comfortably fit all 12 strings. The guitar is played like a regular 6-string model since the strings are tuned to the same notes. On a 12-string guitar there are six sets of strings, two strings to a set. Each set is tuned to the corresponding set on a 6-string guitar; however, the 3rd, 4th, 5th, and 6th sets have an octave spread. While this style of guitar is excellent for folk and blues playing, it is bulkier and less mobile technically. It is not recommended, therefore, that a student begin with this type of guitar.

ARCH-TOP – This type of guitar gets its name from the curved (arched) top on the instrument. Both the front and back of this type of guitar are arched. Modern arch-top guitars usually contain "F"-shaped sound holes. The curvature of the front and back lend a degree of mellowness to the sound. The "F" holes tend to project the sound for greater distances than a comparable round-hole model. Arch-top guitars find much usage as rhythm instruments in dance bands and in country music. Most folk and fingerstyle players prefer the immediate full spread of sound found on round-hole models. Arch-top guitars have metal strings and are usually played with an electric pick-up.

SOLID-BODY ELECTRIC – This is the type of guitar found in most of today's rock and blues music. It is built for speed and amplification. The sound possibilities are endless, depending on the pick-up, tone, and amplifier combination chosen.

HOLLOW-BODY ELECTRIC – This type of guitar is also found in much of today's popular music. Again, the sound possibilities vary according to the electric components selected. Many jazz guitarists prefer an acoustic electric with a deep body. (Essentially, this is an arch-top guitar with an electric pick-up mounted on it.) A mellow tone can result from this combination, but the type of electrical pick-up and amplifier influence this.

ACOUSTIC ELECTRIC – This is an acoustic guitar (nylon or steel string) which has been equipped with a pick-up so it can be plugged into an amplifier. This type of guitar may be played unamplified or amplified.

Parts of the Guitar

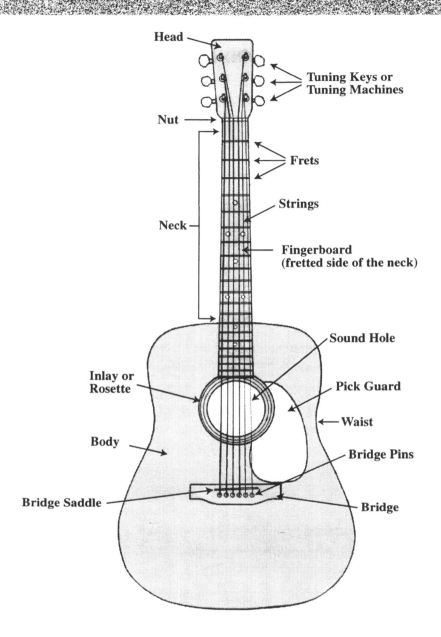

Care of the Guitar

Here are some tips to keep in mind for taking care of the guitar:

1) Make sure the correct type of strings are on the guitar. There are basically two types of strings: nylon and steel. Nylon strings are for the classical guitar and steel strings are for the steel string acoustic (folk) guitar and electric guitar (unless the electric has an "acoustic" pick-up). Steel strings which are bronze are for the steel string acoustic guitar. Bronze strings do not work well on electric guitars unless the electric has an "acoustic pick-up." Most guitars play best if strung with medium or light gauge strings. Heavy gauge strings may warp the neck on some guitars.

2) Avoid rapid temperature and/or humidity changes. A rapid change could damage the finish and the wood of the guitar. Do not leave the guitar in a car when the weather is very hot or cold, and try not to leave the guitar next to heater vents or air conditioners. If the climate is extremely dry, a guitar humidifier can be purchased and used to prevent the guitar drying and cracking.

3) Polish the guitar. Polish which is made specifically for guitars can be purchased from a music store. Besides keeping the guitar looking nice, polishing the guitar will help to protect the finish and the woods. Be careful not to polish the fingerboard.

4) If the guitar is being shipped or taken on an airplane, be sure to loosen the strings. The strings do not have to be completely loose, but loosened considerably so the tension of the strings pulling on the neck is greatly reduced.

Holding Position

Folk or Jazz Position

If the guitar is held properly, it will feel comfortable to you. Although there are many ways to hold the guitar, there are basically two sitting positions: the folk or jazz and the classical positions. Either position may be used, but for most of the material contained in this book, the folk sitting position is recommended.

In the *folk or jazz sitting position,* the guitar is held with the waist of the guitar resting on the right leg. The side of the guitar sits flat on the leg with the neck extending to the left. The neck should be tilted upward slightly so the left arm *does not* rest on the left leg. Both feet should be flat on the floor, although many guitarists prefer to elevate the right leg by using a footstool. The right arm rests on the top of the guitar just beyond the elbow. The right hand should be placed over and to the back (towards the bridge) of the sound hole. Whether using a pick or the fingers, the right-hand fingers should be bent slightly. The right-hand fingers may touch the top of the guitar, but they should not be stationary. They move when stroking the strings.

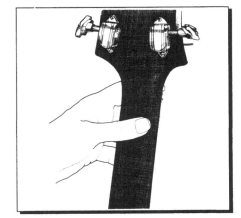

In the *classical sitting position,* the left foot is elevated (with a foot stool), and the guitar rests on the left leg. The body of the guitar also rests on the inside of the right leg. The body of the guitar should rest flat on the left leg. The neck of the guitar should be on about a 45° angle. The right arm rests on the top of the guitar just beyond the elbow. The right hand should be placed to the back (towards the bridge) of the sound hole. Lean forward slightly, touching the top/back of the guitar body. Sit so the right foot is pointing forward.

Classical Position

The left hand should be positioned with the thumb touching the back of the guitar neck. Do not bend the thumb forward. The thumb should be vertical, touching the neck at the knuckle. Do not position the thumb parallel with the neck. The palm of the left hand should not touch the guitar neck. The left wrist may bend *slightly*, but be careful not to exaggerate the bend.

Left-Hand Thumb

When placing a left-hand finger on the string, "square" the finger and push on the string using the tip of the finger. (The fingernails must be short so the tip of the finger can be used.) The finger should be positioned just behind and touching (when possible) the fret wire. Placing the finger too low in the fret may result in a buzz, and placing the finger on top of the fret wire may cause a muted sound. The left-hand knuckles should run parallel with the guitar neck. This makes it possible to reach higher frets with the left-hand third and fourth fingers without turning the wrist. Again, be careful not to bring the left-hand thumb over the top of the guitar neck, and do not touch the guitar neck with the palm of the hand. When pushing on the string, it is as though the guitar neck and string are being pinched between the thumb and finger.

Push the string firmly enough to get a sound, but don't over push. To determine the correct amount of pressure, touch the string with the left-hand finger and gradually apply pressure. Pick the string over and over. When a clear sound occurs, that's the amount of pressure to use.

Fingering Notes

Rest your right-hand thumb on the first (the smallest) string and stroke the open string (open means no left-hand fingers are pushing on the string) downward. Make sure the right-hand wrist moves, and the arm moves slightly from the elbow. The right-hand fingers may touch the top of the guitar, but they should move when the string is played. Try to have a relaxed feeling in the right hand. Go straight down with the thumb when stroking the string. Next, with the right-hand thumb, play the second string open. When playing a string other than the first string, the thumb should go straight down and rest upon (but not play) the next smallest string. In classic guitar playing, this is called a **rest stroke.**

Strumming refers to playing three or more strings so the strings sound simultaneously. To practice the strumming action, rest the right-hand thumb on the fourth string and strum four strings. Using a down stroke, let the right hand fall quickly across the strings so they sound at the same time. The right-hand wrist and arm move with the action.

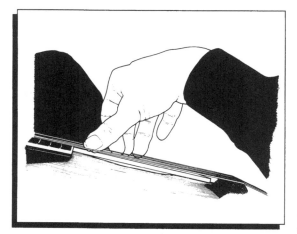

When playing fingerstyle (without a pick), the position of the right hand is very important to achieving a good sound. The right hand should be placed over the rear (towards the bridge) portion of the sound hole. The right-hand fingers should be relaxed and curled in the same manner in which they would be if you were walking. When stroking the string, the tip of the thumb and/or fingers should strike the string first, followed by the tip of the fingernail. This motion should happen quickly so it sounds as if the finger and nail are striking the string at the same time.

Avoid bending the thumb at the first knuckle (the knuckle closest to the nail). Bend the thumb from the joint closest to the palm of the hand. The first knuckle of the fingers should not bend. The movement of the fingers should be restricted to the joint closest to the palm of the right hand and the middle knuckle. When picking up with the fingers, use an up and slightly outward motion. Play one string at a time, and avoid hitting the string next to the one being played. Be careful not to pull the string away from the guitar. This will cause a "flappy, twang" sound. When picking with the thumb, go down and out slightly. Again, avoid pulling the string away from the guitar, and after striking a string, avoid hitting the string next to it.

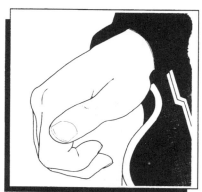

To hold the pick correctly, first, bend the right-hand index finger. The other fingers of the right hand also bend, but not as much as the index finger.

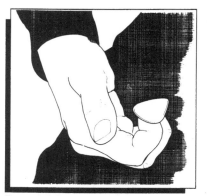

The pick is placed on the end of the index finger with the pointed part of the pick aiming away from the index finger.

The thumb is placed over the pick, covering $2/3$ to $3/4$ of the pick.

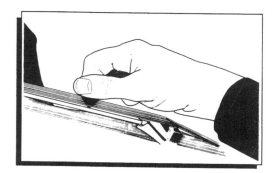

To place the right hand (with the pick) in playing position, rest the pick on the first string. The pick should be tilted upward slightly, rather than at a direct right angle to the string. The pick should stroke the string just over and to the back (towards the bridge) of the sound hole. Pick the first string down. The right-hand wrist should move slightly when the string is played, and the right arm should move slightly from the elbow. When playing strings other than the first, after stroking the string, the pick should rest on the next smallest string. This action is a type of **rest stroke,** which is commonly used in fingerstyle playing, and will generate a richer and fuller tone than picking with an outward motion will. Try playing each of the strings using this type of motion.

To get the feel of strumming with the pick, rest the pick on the fourth string and strum four strings down. Be sure to have a relaxed right hand. Move the wrist and arm slightly when doing the strumming. When picking a single string, or strumming, upward, the pick is tilted down slightly so the pick will glide across the strings, rather than "bite" or snag them.

Tuning

There are several methods which can be used to tune the guitar. One way to tune the guitar is to tune it to itself. You can tune the first string of the guitar to a piano, pitch pipe, tuning fork, or some other instrument, and then match the strings to each other. To do this, use the following steps:

▶ 1. Tune the first open string to an E note. (Remember, open means that no left-hand fingers are pushing on the string.) You can use a piano, pitch pipe, tuning fork, or another instrument. If you use a tuning fork, use an "E" tuning fork. Hold the fork at the bass and tap the fork on your knee, or another object, to get the fork to vibrate. Then, touch the bass of the fork near the bottom of the bridge of the guitar. The pitch which will sound is the pitch the first string should have when the string is played open.

▶ 2. After the first string is tuned, place a left-hand finger on the second string in the fifth fret. Play the first and second strings together. They should be the same pitch. If not, adjust the second string to match the first.

▶ 3. Place a finger on the third string in the fourth fret. The third string should now sound the same as the second string open. If not, adjust the third string.

▶ 4. Place a finger on the fourth string in the fifth fret. The fourth string, fifth fret should sound the same as the third string open.

▶ 5. Place a finger on the fifth string, fifth fret. This should sound the same as the fourth string open.

▶ 6. Place a finger on the sixth string, fifth fret. The sixth string, fifth fret should sound the same as the fifth string, open.

The diagram below shows where the fingers are placed to tune the guitar to itself.

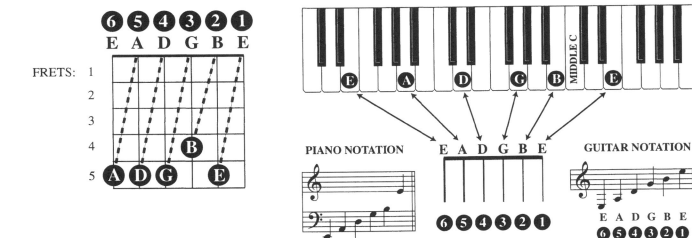

Another common method of tuning is the use of an *electric tuner*. Tuners utilize lights (LEDs) or Vu meters to indicate if a string is sharp or flat. Tuners have built in microphones or electric guitars can be plugged in directly. Follow the instructions provided with the tuner. If the tuner does not respond to playing a string, make sure you are playing the correct string and, if it is adjustable, the tuner is set for that particular string. Sometimes on the lower notes, the tuner won't function properly. If this happens, try playing the harmonic on the twelfth fret of the string. To do this, place a left-hand finger on the string over the twelfth fret-wire. Touch (do not push) the string very lightly. Pick the string. A note should be heard which will have a "chime" effect. This is a harmonic. It will ring longer if the left-hand finger is moved away from the string soon after it is picked. The electric tuner will most likely respond to this note.

Reading the Music Diagrams

The music in this book will be written using chord diagrams, tablature, and standard notation.

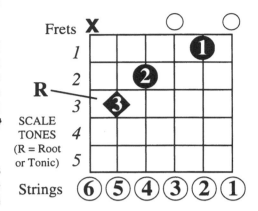

Chord diagrams will be used to illustrate chords and scales. With the chord diagrams, the vertical lines represent the strings on the guitar, with the first string being on the right. The horizontal lines represent frets, with the first fret being on the top. Dots, or numbers, on the lines show the placement of left-hand fingers. The numbers on, or next to the dots indicate which left-hand finger to use. A diamond may be used to indicate the placement of the root of the chord or scale. *Root* refers to a note which has the same letter name as the chord or scale.

A zero above a string indicates the string is to be played open (no left-hand fingers are pushing on the string). An "X" above a string indicates that string is not to be played, or that the string is to be muted by tilting one of the left-hand fingers and touching the string lightly.

Left-Hand Fingers

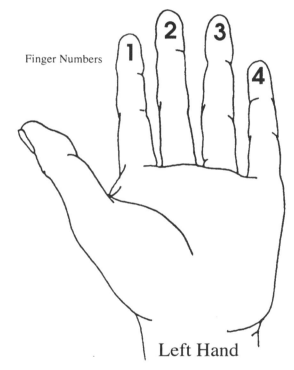

Left Hand

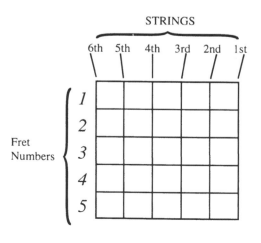

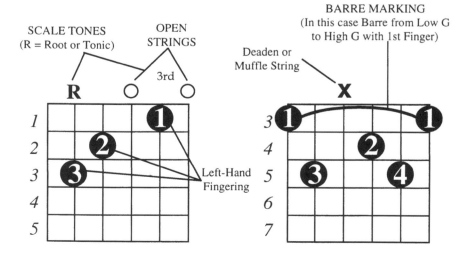

First Warm-Up

To become familiar with the feel of the guitar, and to develop coordination, do the following warm-up exercise:

Step 1

Begin by playing the first string, open. **Open** means no left-hand fingers are pushing on the string.

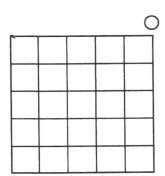

Step 2

Next, play the first string, first fret. The left-hand first finger should be pushing on the string. Be sure to get a good, clear sound.

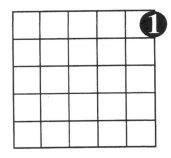

Step 3

Next, play the first string, second fret. The left-hand second finger should be used to push on the second fret.

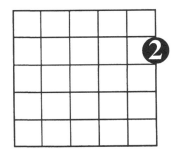

Step 4

Next, play the first string, third fret, using the left-hand third finger.

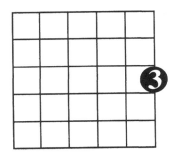

Step 5

Finally, play the first string, fourth fret, using the left-hand fourth finger.

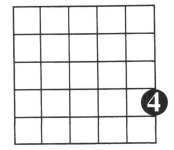

Now, play these same notes in the reverse order (4-3-2-1), still on the first string. Repeat this exercise several times up and down the fingerboard. Notice that the same number left-hand finger is used as the fret number. After doing the exercise several times on the first string, repeat the same sequence on each string.

Solos by Number

All of the music in this text should be played with a pick or with the right hand thumb unless noted otherwise.

Top Number = Fret
Botton Number = String

Boil That Cabbage

 Disc 1
Track #2

Southern American Song

Fret:	0	0	0	0	1	1	1	1	0	0	0	0	3	Pause
String:	1	1	1	1	1	1	1	1	1	1	1	1	2	

Fret:	0	0	0	0	1	1	1	1	0	0	3	3	1	Pause
String:	1	1	1	1	1	1	1	1	1	1	2	2	2	

Lightly Row

 Disc 1
Track #3

Fret:	3	0	0	Pause	1	3	3	Pause	1	3	0	1	3	3	3	Pause
String:	1	1	1		1	2	2		2	2	1	1	1	1	1	

Fret:	3	0	0	Pause	1	3	3	Pause	1	0	3	3	0	Pause
String:	1	1	1		1	2	2		2	1	1	1	1	

Fret:	3	3	3	3	3	0	1	Pause	0	0	0	0	0	1	3	Pause
String:	2	2	2	2	2	1	1		1	1	1	1	1	1	1	

Fret:	3	0	0	0	1	3	3	3	1	0	3	3	1	Pause
String:	1	1	1	1	1	2	2	2	2	1	1	1	2	

Mozart's Theme
(Also known as *Twinkle, Twinkle Little Star*)

 Disc 1
Track #4

Fret:	0	0	3	3	0	0	3	___	1	1	0	0	2	2	0	___
String:	3	3	2	2	1	1	2		2	2	2	2	3	3	3	

Fret:	0	0	3	3	0	0	3	___	1	1	0	0	2	2	0	___
String:	3	3	2	2	1	1	2		2	2	2	2	3	3	3	

Fret:	3	3	1	1	0	0	2	___	3	3	1	1	0	0	2	___
String:	2	2	2	2	2	2	3		2	2	2	2	2	2	3	

Fret:	0	0	3	3	0	0	3	___	1	1	0	0	2	2	0	___
String:	3	3	2	2	1	1	2		2	2	2	2	3	3	3	

Wolfgang Amadeus Mozart (1756-1791)

Mozart showed amazing musical talent at a very young age. Mozart began composing at the age of five. His father, Leopold, decided to commercialize his talent and set up concert tours that included playing for royalty.

AUSTRIA

Simple Chords

If three or more strings are played at the same time, this is called a **chord**. Drawn on the diagram below is the simple G chord. This chord may also be referred to as G major. Major chords are those which are written with a letter name only. That is, they will not have an "m" or numbers written after the letter name. Remember, zero above a string indicates the string is to be played open, and an "X" indicates the string is not to be played. Be careful to use the correct left-hand finger. Use the right-hand thumb or a pick to strum the chords. Be sure to strum straight down using a combination of the wrist and elbow.

These two signs, (╱ and ⌐), are called strum bars. They indicate the chord is to be strummed down one time. Each strum bar gets one beat. This sign, (⊓), when written above a strum bar, (⌐), confirms that the strum is to be strummed down. Up strums will be presented later in this book.

G Chord – EZ Form

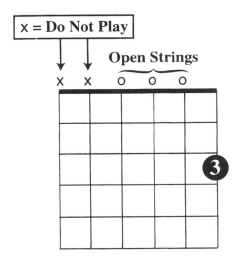

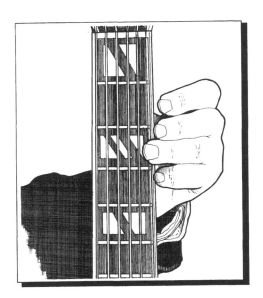

x= Do not play 6th & 7th strings
o= 4th, 3rd & 2nd strings are played open
❸= Press the 3rd finger down on the 3rd fret on the 1st string

① G / / / / / / / /   G / / / / / / / /

Brother John

Disc 1
Track #5

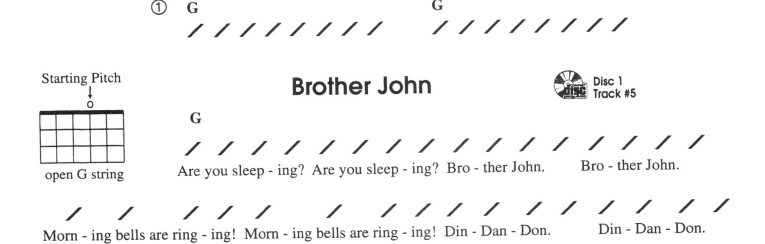

Starting Pitch
open G string

G
/ / / / / / / / / / / /
Are you sleep - ing? Are you sleep - ing? Bro - ther John.   Bro - ther John.

/ / / / / / / / / / / /
Morn - ing bells are ring - ing! Morn - ing bells are ring - ing! Din - Dan - Don.   Din - Dan - Don.

C Chord — EZ Form

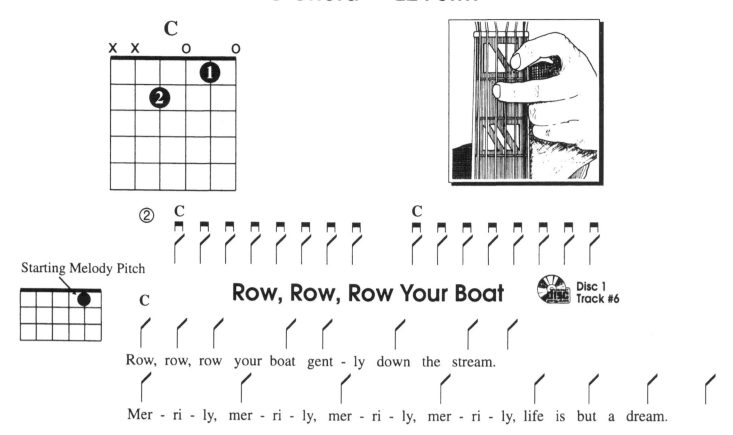

Starting Melody Pitch

Row, Row, Row Your Boat

Disc 1
Track #6

Row, row, row your boat gent - ly down the stream.

Mer - ri - ly, mer - ri - ly, mer - ri - ly, mer - ri - ly, life is but a dream.

Combining Chords

The following exercise uses **G** and **C** chords. Strum each chord the number of times indicated by the strum bars.

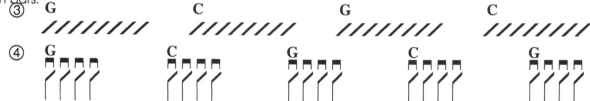

Practice changing from one chord to the next. A technique which will help change chords quickly is to keep the right hand going when changing chords. At first, just play open strings between the chord changes because it will be difficult to change quickly.

But, eventually, the left hand will catch up to the right. Then, the "open-string fill" will go away because the chords

Rock-A-My Soul

Disc 1
Track #7

Spiritual

Starting Melody Pitch

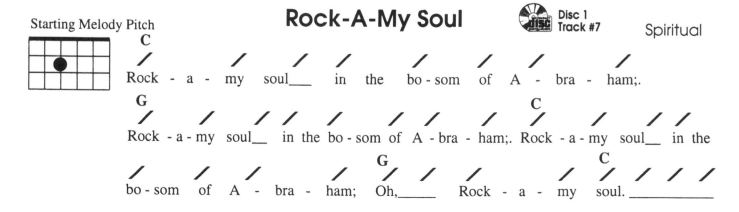

Rock - a - my soul___ in the bo - som of A - bra - ham;.

Rock - a - my soul__ in the bo - som of A - bra - ham;. Rock - a - my soul__ in the

bo - som of A - bra - ham; Oh,____ Rock - a - my soul. _____

G7 Chord - EZ Form

The next chord to learn is simple **G7**.

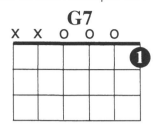

Play the following exercise which contains simple G7.

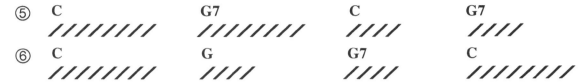

Playing Chords to Measured Music

If a song is in 4/4 time (see p. 21 for the explanation of time signatures), there are four counts in each measure (see p. 19 for the explanation of measures). In 3/4 time, there are three counts in each measure. For 4/4 time, the simplest strum is to strum down four times in each measure. This accompaniment, though simple, will work to play many songs in 4/4. Play the following exercise strumming down four times in each measure. If a chord name is not written above a measure, continue playing the last written chord through that measure.

Because the next exercise is in 3/4, strum down three times in each measure.

Practice playing the following song which is in 4/4. Strum down four times in each measure. When playing the chords to a song from music like this, do not be concerned with the notes. Only be concerned with the chord names, the number of measures each chord gets, and the number of beats in each measure,

Marianne

Disc 1 Track #8

Quiz

① Label the parts of the guitar.

② Draw the chords on the diagram below.

| G — EZ Form | C — EZ Form | G7 — EZ Form |

  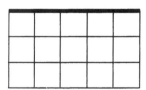

③ Write a chord progression using **C — G — G7** chords

Write chord name

Write in strum marks

Learning to Read Tablature

Tablature is a way of writing guitar music which tells you where to find notes. In tablature:

Lines = Strings
Numbers = Frets

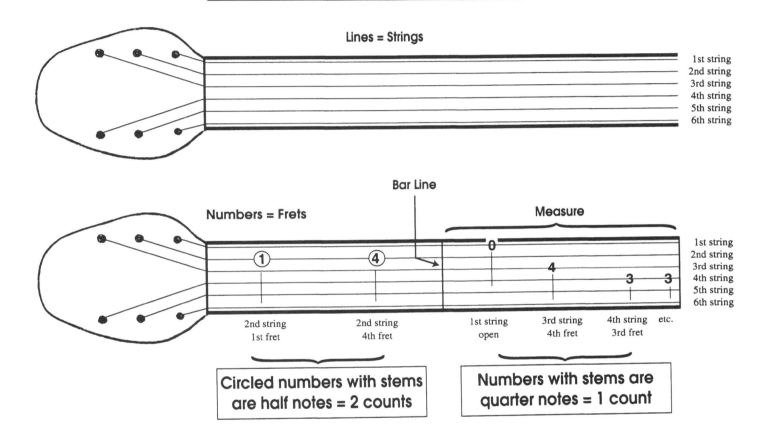

Playing Several Notes at Once

When numbers appear right above one another, more than one string is played at the same time.

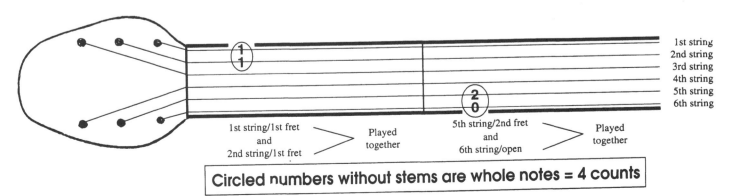

Ludwig Van Beethoven (1772-1827)

Beethoven was one of the world's greatest composers. He was born in Germany in the city of Bonn. Beethoven showed early ability in music, especially the ability to improvise or make up musical themes spontaneously. When Beethoven was approximately 30 years old, he began noticing he was losing his hearing. One of the amazing features about Beethoven was that he continued to compose some of his greatest works while he was deaf. His greatest works are his Nine Symphonies and they are known for the artistic development of the themes and the emotional power conveyed in the music. "Song of Joy" is a theme from his Ninth Symphony.

GERMANY

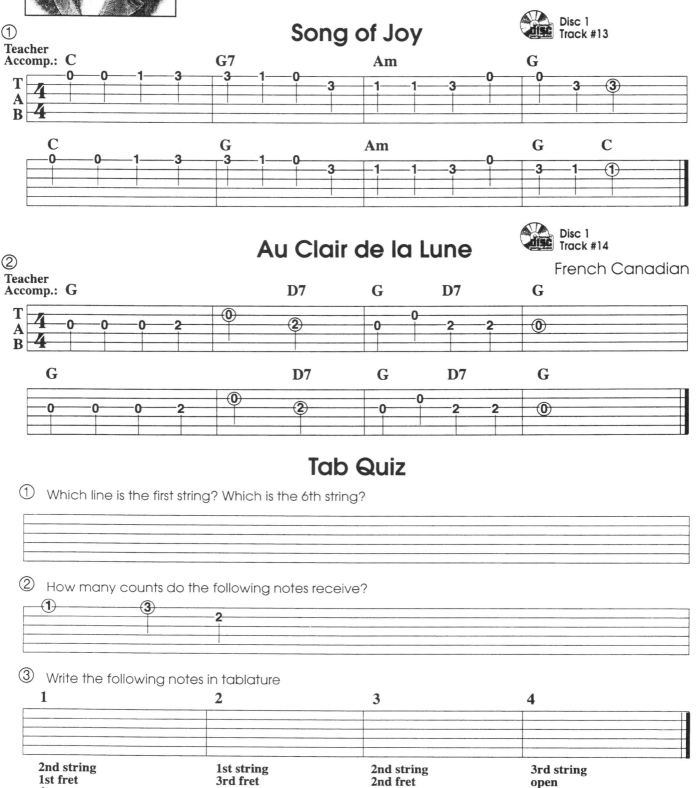

Song of Joy

Disc 1
Track #13

① Teacher Accomp.:

Au Clair de la Lune

Disc 1
Track #14

French Canadian

② Teacher Accomp.:

Tab Quiz

① Which line is the first string? Which is the 6th string?

② How many counts do the following notes receive?

③ Write the following notes in tablature

1	2	3	4
2nd string 1st fret 4 counts	1st string 3rd fret 1 count	2nd string 2nd fret 2 counts	3rd string open 1 count

Guitar Ensemble in Tablature
Guitaround

Disc 1
Track #15

Have the entire class play this round in unison. Then, divide the class in half. Play it again with one half starting at number ① and the other half starting at number ① when the first half reaches number ②.

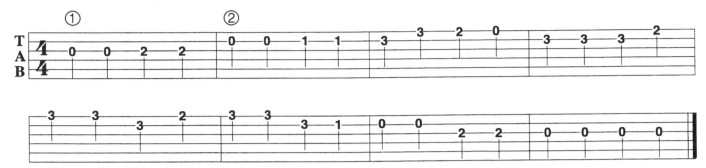

Tab Trio

The following piece is written for three guitars. Divide the class into three sections. Have each section play a part.

Where the Red Fern Grows

Disc 1
Track #16

Arranged by
M. C.

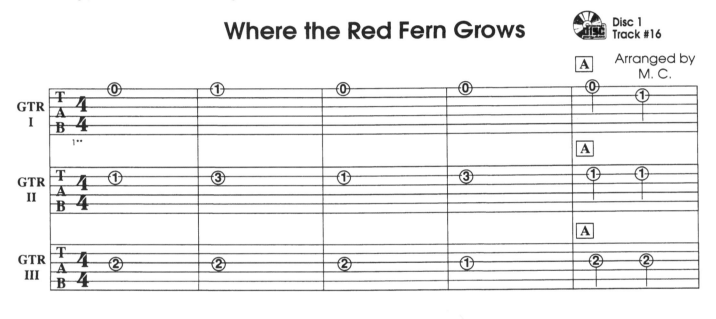

* This is rehearsal que. In rehearsal, the conductor (or a member of the ensemble) may refer to these letters as starting points.

** These are measure numbers.

Reading Standard Notation

The Staff

Music is written on a *staff* consisting of *five lines* and *four spaces.* The lines and spaces are numbered upward as shown.

5TH LINE
4TH LINE   4TH SPACE
3RD LINE   3RD SPACE
2ND LINE   2ND SPACE
1ST LINE   1ST SPACE

The lines and spaces are named after letters of the alphabet.

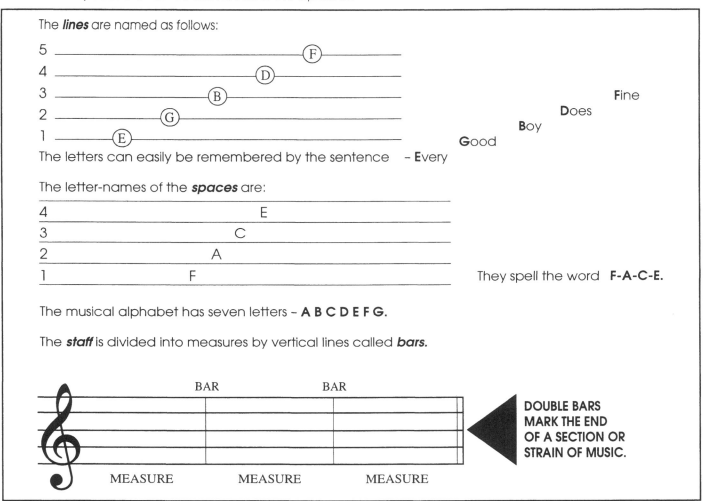

The *lines* are named as follows:

5 — F
4 — D
3 — B
2 — G
1 — E

The letters can easily be remembered by the sentence – **E**very **G**ood **B**oy **D**oes **F**ine

The letter-names of the *spaces* are:

4 — E
3 — C
2 — A
1 — F

They spell the word **F-A-C-E.**

The musical alphabet has seven letters – **A B C D E F G.**

The *staff* is divided into measures by vertical lines called *bars.*

BAR   BAR

MEASURE   MEASURE   MEASURE

DOUBLE BARS MARK THE END OF A SECTION OR STRAIN OF MUSIC.

The Clef

This sign is the treble or G clef.

All guitar music will be written in this clef.

The second line of the treble clef is known as the G line. Many people call the treble clef the G clef because it circles around the G line.

Notes

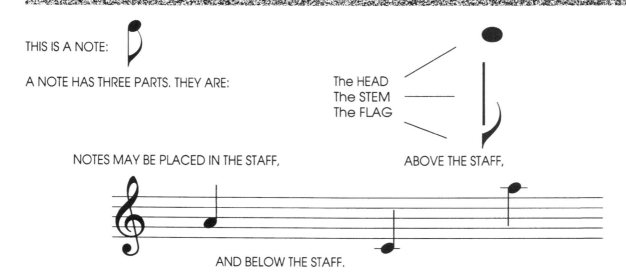

THIS IS A NOTE:

A NOTE HAS THREE PARTS. THEY ARE:

The HEAD
The STEM
The FLAG

NOTES MAY BE PLACED IN THE STAFF,   ABOVE THE STAFF,

AND BELOW THE STAFF.

A note will bear the name of the line or space it occupies on the staff.
The location of a note in, above, or below the staff will indicate the pitch.

PITCH: the height or depth of a tone.
TONE: a musical sound.

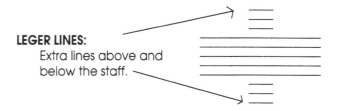

LEGER LINES:
Extra lines above and
below the staff.

Types of Notes

The type of note
will indicate the
length of its sound.

This is a whole note.
The head is hollow.
It does not have a stem.

This is a half note.
The head is hollow.
It has a stem.

This is a quarter note.
The head is solid.
It has a stem.

This is an eighth note.
The head is solid.
It has a stem and a flag.

= 4 Beats
A whole note will receive
four beats or counts.

= 2 Beats
A half note will receive
two beats or counts.

= 1 Beat
A quarter note will receive
one beat or count.

 = $\frac{1}{2}$ Beat
An eighth note will receive
one-half beat or count.
(2 for 1 beat)

Rests

A **rest** is a sign used to designate a period of silence. This period of silence will be of the same duration of time as the note to which it corresponds.

 This is an eighth rest.

 This is a quarter rest.

 Half rest.
(Half rests lie on the line.)

 Whole rest.
(Whole rests hang down from the line.)

Notes

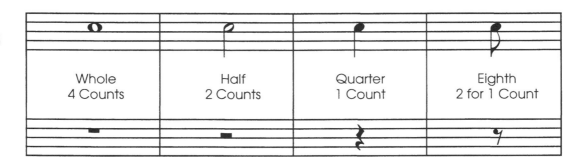

| Whole 4 Counts | Half 2 Counts | Quarter 1 Count | Eighth 2 for 1 Count |

Rests

The Time Signature

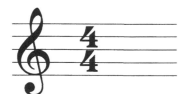  

The above examples are the common types of time signatures to be used in this book.

The number of beats per measure.

 Four beats per measure

The type of note receiving one beat.

 A quarter note receives one beat.

 Signifies so-called **common time** and is simply another way of designating 4/4 time.

Our First Note

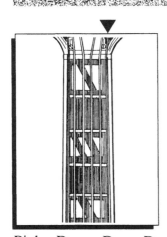

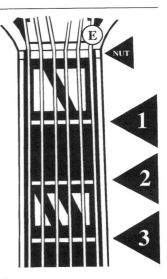

E

The first string on the guitar is called the high E String. **Our first note is E-open 1st string.**

(Open)
Unless otherwise indicated, use a pick to play the exercises and solos in this book. Use a downstroke to play quarter, half, and whole notes.

Disc 1
Track #17

E Study #1

(Use a pick to play the following studies)

Pick: Down Down Down Down

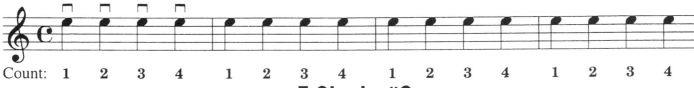

Count: 1   2   3   4   1   2   3   4   1   2   3   4   1   2   3   4

E Study #2

Pick:

Count: 1   2   3   4   1   2   3 4

E Study #3

Count: 1 2   3   4   1 2   3   4

E Study #4

Count: 1   2   3   4   1   2   3   4   1   2   3   4   1   2   3   4

E Study #5

Pick:

Count: 1   2 3   4

$\frac{3}{4}$ Time

In 3/4 time we have three beats per measure.

E in $\frac{3}{4}$ Time

Disc 1
Track #18

Pick: down   down   down

Count: 1   2   3   1   2   3

#2

Pick:

Count: 1   2   3   1   2 3

#3

Pick:

Count: 1   2 3   1 2   3

Eighth Note Review/Alternate Picking

Shown below are eighth notes and their time values:

Eighth Notes get ¹/₂ beat if the bottom number of the time signature is a four.

one   and

One beat. The beat is divided equally into two parts. Count the first eighth note as the beat in the measure on which it happens, and count the second eighth note as "and."

When two eighth notes are connected, the first is played using a downstroke, ⊓ , and the second is played using an upstroke, ∨ . This is called **alternate picking.** This technique is used regardless of the position or the string on which the note is played. **Use alternate picking on all eighth notes throughout this book, unless otherwise indicated.** When tapping your foot, the first eighth note is played down when the foot is down, and the second eighth note is played up when the foot is up.

Play the following exercise which contains eighth notes, alternate picking, and the E note on the first string. Be sure to count and tap your foot.

Hiking Up the Mountain

Disc 1
Track #19

Say: Hi-king up the moun-tain, Hi-king up the moun-tain

Try clapping the rhythm while you say the rhythmic phrase.

Study #1

(Say and Play)

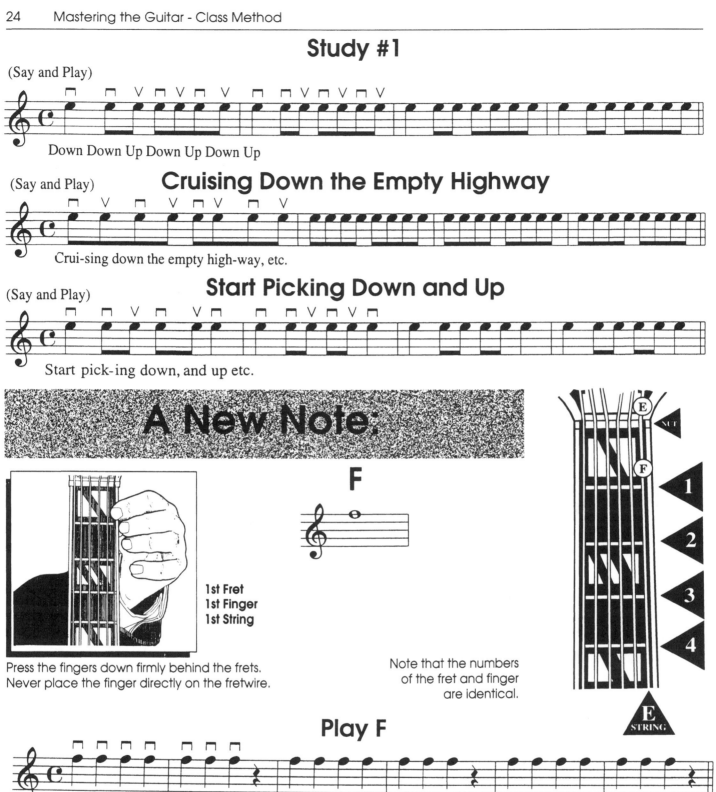

Down Down Up Down Up Down Up

Cruising Down the Empty Highway

(Say and Play)

Crui-sing down the empty high-way, etc.

Start Picking Down and Up

(Say and Play)

Start pick-ing down, and up etc.

A New Note:

F

1st Fret
1st Finger
1st String

Press the fingers down firmly behind the frets.
Never place the finger directly on the fretwire.

Note that the numbers
of the fret and finger
are identical.

E
NUT
F
1
2
3
4
E STRING

Play F

E-F

E-F in $\frac{3}{4}$ Time

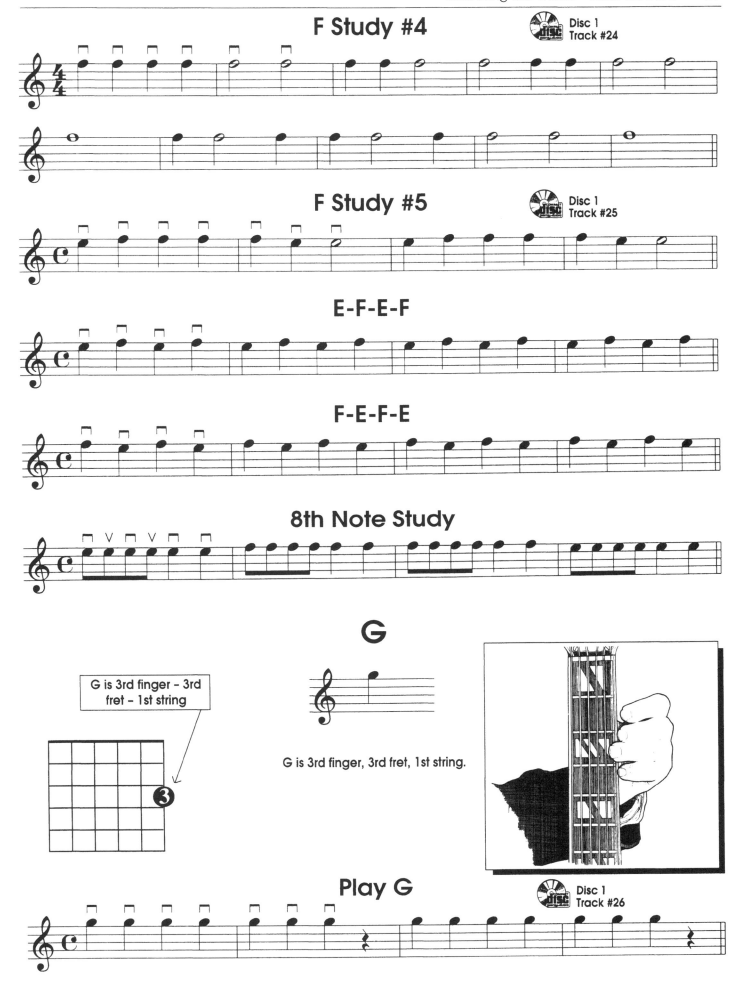

F Study #4

Disc 1
Track #24

F Study #5

Disc 1
Track #25

E-F-E-F

F-E-F-E

8th Note Study

G

G is 3rd finger – 3rd
fret – 1st string

G is 3rd finger, 3rd fret, 1st string.

Play G

Disc 1
Track #26

1st String Studies
8th Note Rhythm

Disc 1
Track #31

Study #2

Picking Study

Disc 1
Track #32

Time and Picking Study

Disc 1
Track #33

Play Slowly

Speed Study

Disc 1
Track #34

Music and Math Quiz

Grade _____

a. Write how many beats the notes or rests would receive.

$\mathbf{o}$ = _____ Beats

$\boldsymbol{\sigma}$ = _____ Beats

$\boldsymbol{\downarrow}$ = _____ Beats

$\boldsymbol{\downarrow}$ = _____ Beats

$\blacksquare$ = _____ Beats

$\boldsymbol{\xi}$ = _____ Beats

$\blacksquare$ = _____ Beats

$\boldsymbol{\gamma}$ = _____ Beats

b. Write the answer to the following addition problems.

1. $\sigma + \sigma$ =

2. $\downarrow + \downarrow + \sigma$ =

3. $\mathbf{o} + \sigma$ =

4. $\mathbf{o} + \mathbf{o}$ =

5. $\downarrow + \mathbf{o} + \sigma$ =

6. $\mathbf{o} + \downarrow$ =

7. $\sigma + \sigma + \downarrow$ =

8. $\downarrow + \mathbf{o}$ =

9. $\sigma + \downarrow + \sigma$ =

10. $\mathbf{o} + \sigma + \downarrow$ =

11. $\sigma + \sigma + \blacksquare$ =

12. $\downarrow + \downarrow$ =

13. $\sigma + \blacksquare$ =

14. $\mathbf{o} + \xi$ =

15. $\gamma + \gamma + \xi$ =

16. $\blacksquare + \sigma$ =

17. $\gamma + \gamma + \gamma + \blacksquare$ =

18. $\sigma + \mathbf{o} + \downarrow + \xi + \blacksquare$ =

B

B is 2nd string – open.

B is 2nd string, open.

B Study

Disc 1
Track #35

B Study #2

B – E

C

C is 1st fret –
1st finger – 2nd string

C is 1st finger,
1st fret, 2nd string.

C Study

Disc 1
Track #36

B – C – C – B

$\frac{3}{4}$ C – B

D

D is 3rd finger, 3rd fret, 2nd string.

Play D

D – B – C

D – C – B

Using All the Notes

C – B – C

Three Fishermen

Disc 1 Track #40

Secret Garden

Disc 1 Track #41

Rock Feeling

Disc 1 Track #42

Drivin' Pick

Disc 1 Track #43

Speed Study

Disc 1 Track #44

*mf mezzo forte - medium loud (see p. 131)

The Tie

Disc 1
Track #45

A **tie** is a curved line that connects two notes of the same pitch. *With a tie, you pick only the first note.*

If the first end of the two eighth notes is tied, don't play the first note, but play the second note using an upstroke.

Let this eighth note ring through the time value of the next eighth note.

Practice the following exercise containing ties.

Dotted Half Note

A dotted half note receives 3 beats.

Study

Disc 1
Track #46

Cmaj7   Dm   C   Dm   C   G   C

In tablature a circled number with a dot receives 3 beats.

Sing Down the Moon

Disc 1
Track #47

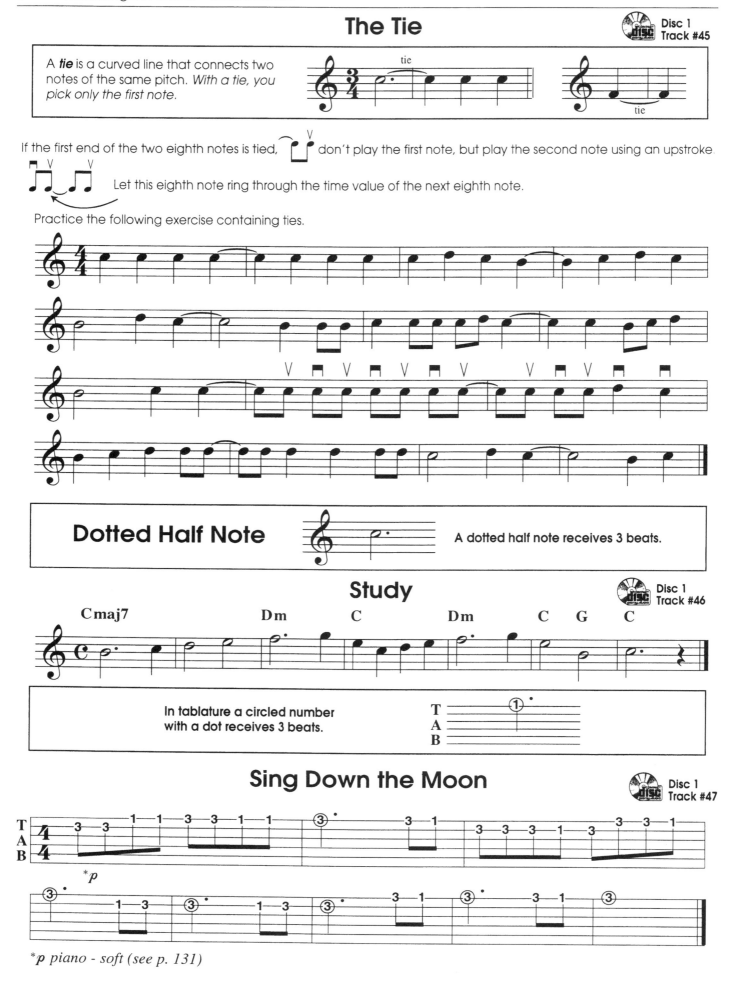

*p piano - soft (see p. 131)

Musical Math Quiz

Grade _____

Write the answers to the following addition problems.

1. 𝅗𝅥 + 𝅗𝅥 =
2. 𝅗𝅥 + 𝅗𝅥. =
3. 𝅝 + 𝅗𝅥 =
4. 𝅗𝅥. + ♩ =
5. 𝅗𝅥. + 𝅗𝅥. =

6. 𝅝 + 𝅗𝅥. =
7. 𝅗𝅥. + 𝅗𝅥 =
8. 𝅝 + 𝅝 =
9. 𝅗𝅥. + 𝅝 =
10. 𝅝 + ♩ =

11. ♩ + ♩ + 𝅗𝅥 =
12. 𝅗𝅥 + ♩ + 𝅗𝅥. =
13. 𝅗𝅥. + 𝅗𝅥 + ♩ =
14. ♩ + 𝅝 + 𝅗𝅥 =

15. 𝅝 + 𝅗𝅥. + ♩ =
16. 𝅗𝅥. + ♩ + 𝅗𝅥 =
17. ♩ + 𝅝 + ♩ =
18. 𝅝 + 𝅗𝅥. + 𝅝 =

Notes on the 3rd String

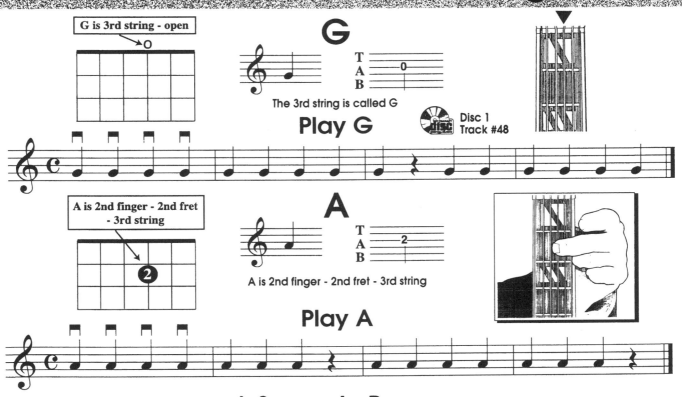

The 3rd string is called G

Play G

Disc 1 Track #48

A is 2nd finger - 2nd fret - 3rd string

Play A

A Separate Peace

Suggested reading: *A Separate Peace* by John Knowles

Disc 1 Track #49

⌢ fermata - pause, hold

A Wrinkle In Time
Guitar Ensemble in Three Parts

Disc 1
Track #50

Arranged by
M. C.

*Andante - walking speed (see p. 131)
**tempo indication - set metronome at 108 (108 beats per minute)
***crescendo - gradually get louder (see p. 131)
****ritardando (rit.) - gradually get slower (see p. 131)

Review of the First 3 Strings

Running the Strings

Disc 1
Track #51

The Hobbit

Disc 1
Track #52

My Side of the Mountain

Disc 1
Track #53

Swamp Buggy

Disc 1
Track #54

* Pick-up notes are notes leading into the downbeat of the first measure of a song.

f forte - loud (see p. 131)

Solos on the First 3 Strings
Renaissance Dance Disc 1 Track #55

Renaissance Period - The Renaissance was a period from roughly 1450 - 1600. Renaissance means "Rebirth." It was a period where there was great interest in art, music, and science. Can you name some famous people of the Renaissance?

Chanson
(Chanson is French for Song) Disc 1 Track #56

Sourwood Mountain Disc 1 Track #57   Fiddle Tune

Oh, Sinner Man Disc 1 Track #58   Southern Spiritual

Shadow of the Bull
Guitar Ensemble in Three Parts

Suggested reading: *Shadow of a Bull* by Wojciechowska

Disc 1
Track #59

Arranged by
M. C.

*de crescendo - gradually get softer (see p. 131)

**pp - very soft (see p. 131)

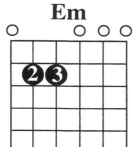

Em

E Minor

The chord drawn at left is E minor. **Minor** chords are written with an **m** or a **dash (-)** next to the chord letter name.

Disc 1
Track #60

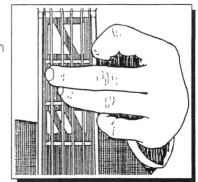

Practice the following exercise which contains E minor.

① Em   C   Em

G   Em

This is a three beat strum. Strum the chord on the first beat and let it ring for two more beats.

D

D

X X ○

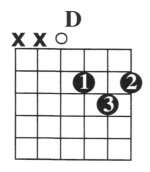

Drawn at left is the **D chord.** Practice getting a clear sound out of each of the strings in a D chord. Notice only four strings are played.

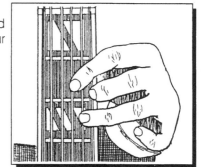

Practice the following exercises which contain some D chords. Notice the use of rests in this exercise.

② D   C   G

D   D   C   G   D

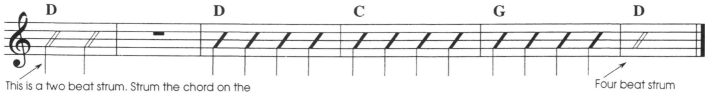

This is a two beat strum. Strum the chord on the first beat and let it ring through the second beat.

Four beat strum

③ Em   D   C   G   Em

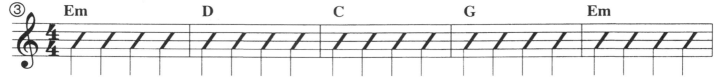

D   C   D   Em

Practice the following songs using the chords you have learned so far. Above the first measure in each song is written the number of times to strum in each measure.

The Cuckoo

Disc 1
Track #61

> : This is an **accent mark.** When it is placed above a note or a strum bar, play that note or strum slightly louder.

Sweet Sunny South

Disc 1
Track #62

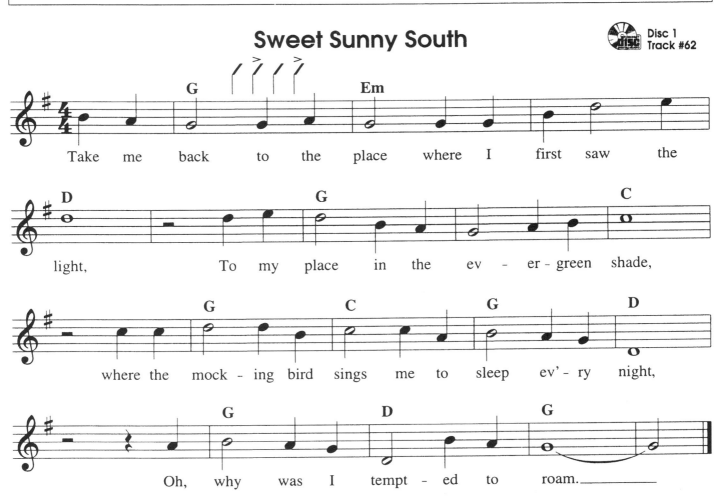

Full G, G7, and C Chords

 Disc 1
Track #63

Drawn below are the full **G, G7, and C chords.** These full chords will sound better than the simple chords and should be used from here on throughout this book. To get a clear sound out of each string, keep the knuckles square and use the tips of the fingers. On the G chord, the numbers in parenthesis are an optional fingering.

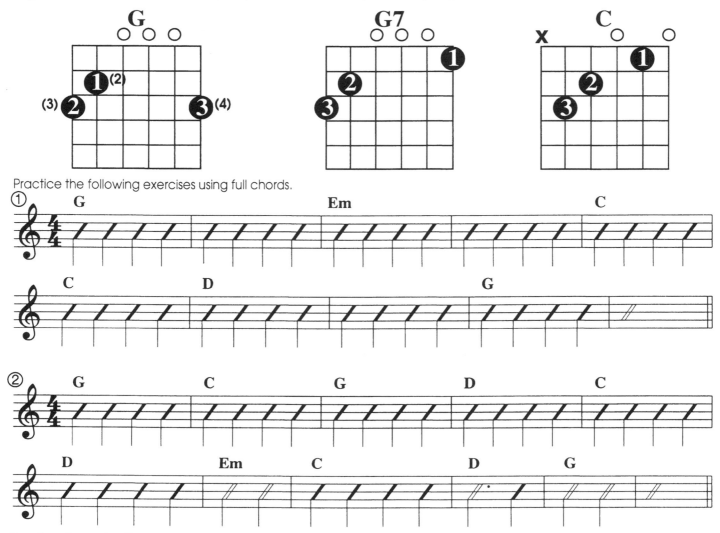

Practice the following exercises using full chords.

Practice strumming the chords to the following song using full chords.

Will the Circle Be Unbroken?

 Disc 1
Track #64

Will the cir - cle _____ be un - bro - ken _____ by and
by Lord, by and by, _____ There's a bet - ter _____ home a -
wai - tin' _____ in the sky Lord, in the - sky. _____

Strum Patterns

Disc 1
Track #65

Like eighth notes, when two strum bars are connected with a beam, [symbol], two strums are played in one beat. Usually, the first strum is down, and the second is strummed up, [symbol]. The down-up strum is counted the same as two eighth notes (i.e. "one-and"). As with the down strums, the strumming may be done with a pick, the right-hand thumb, or the first finger. When strumming up, only the first (smallest) two or three strings should be strummed. The up strum is done quickly with an up and outward motion.

Practice the following using down-up strums.

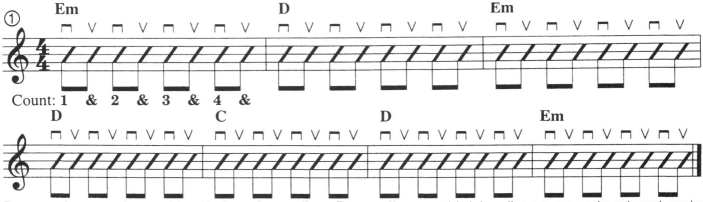

Down-up strums can be combined to form **strum patterns.** These patterns provide interesting accompaniments and can be used to play many songs. One pattern which can be used to accompany songs in 4/4 is: [symbol].

This pattern can be used to play each measure of any song in 4/4. The songs and exercises in this book which are to be strummed will have strum patterns written above (or in) the first measure. That pattern should be used in each measure of the song, unless otherwise indicated. It's important to realize that these patterns can not only be used to play the songs in this book, but they can also be applied to songs in 4/4 and 3/4 from sheet music and/or songbooks.

Practice the following exercise and song repeating the strum pattern which is written above (or in) the first measure.

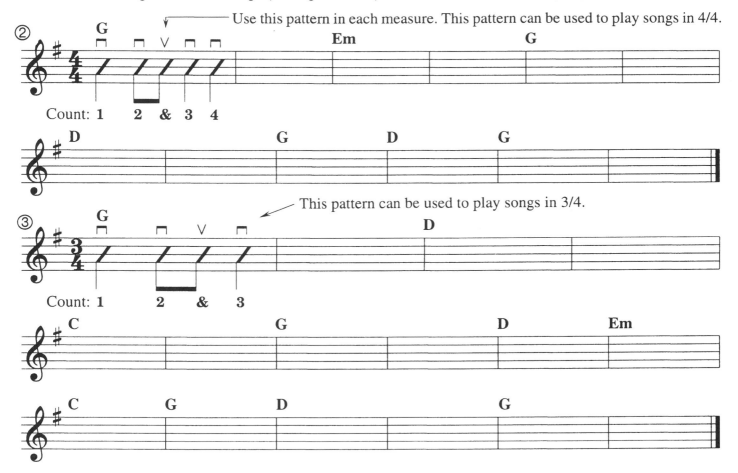

Swing Rhythm

When strumming chords, it is common to play eighth note strums (two strums to a beat) using *swing rhythm*. When playing swing rhythm, rather than divide each beat into two equal parts, the beat is divided into a long-short pattern:

Long ⟶ ⟵ Short
(2/3 beat)   (1/3 beat)

The down strum note gets about 2/3 of the beat and the up strum gets about 1/3 of the beat. This rhythm gives the music a bouncy feel. To get the feel of this rhythm, think of the melody to the "Battle Hymn of the Republic." This song is often sung with a swing feel.

Power chords, which are presented later in this book, are often played using swing rhythm.

Songs in 3/4 Time
Amazing Grace

Disc 1
Track #68

Hymn

A - maz - ing Grace, how sweet the sound that saved a wretch like me. I once was lost but now am found, was blind but now I see.

The Railroad Corral

Disc 1
Track #69

AMERICAN COWBOY SONG

Written in 1904 by Joseph Mills Hansen and based on the tune of a Scottish ballad called "Bonnie Dundee."

We're up in the morn - ing at break - ing of day. The chuck wa - gon's bu - sy, the flap - jacks in play. The herd is a stir o - ver hill - side and vale, with the night rid - ers crowd - ing them on - to the trail.

Jargon: Specialized vocabulary for a specific activity, sport, profession, etc.

chuck wagon	bronco
flapjacks	roust
cinches	chaparral
reins	corral

CHORUS:
Come take up your cinches and shake out your reins, (G) (C) (G)
Come wake your old bronco and break for the plains. (C) (G)
Come roust out your steers from the long chaparral, (C) (D)
For the outfit is off to the railroad corral. (G) (C) (G)

New Strum Pattern

Disc 1
Track #70

The pattern shown in the first measure works well with songs in 4/4 time. Remember to use the same strum pattern in every measure.

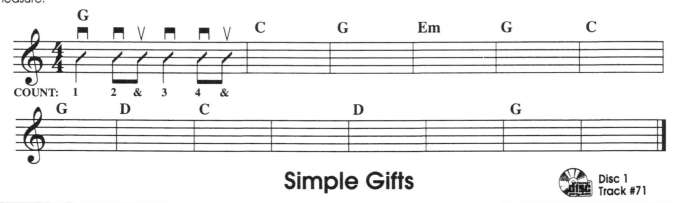

Simple Gifts

Disc 1
Track #71

"Simple Gifts" is the most famous song of a historical American religious sect known as the Shakers. This song was used by American composer Aaron Copland as the theme of his ballet suite "Appalachian Spring." The Shakers began their sect in England in about 1706 but later, in 1774 under the leadership of Anne Lee, established a community in Watervliet, New York. The Shakers believed in a simple, communal lifestyle. All property was owned by the community. They invented the circular saw, cut nails, a washing machine, metal pen points and designed a style of furniture still popular today.

*(1) **Alternate #1**. We will discuss playing two different chords in one measure later on page 80. Try these alternate measures to add color to the ending phrases. What is different about these alternate endings?

Two More Strum Patterns in 4/4 Time

Disc 1
Track #72

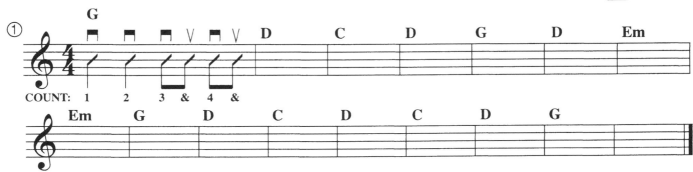

Disc 1
Track #73

The Cruel War

Suggested reading: *The Red Badge of Courage* by Stephen Crane (a story about the American Civil War.)

English Ballad

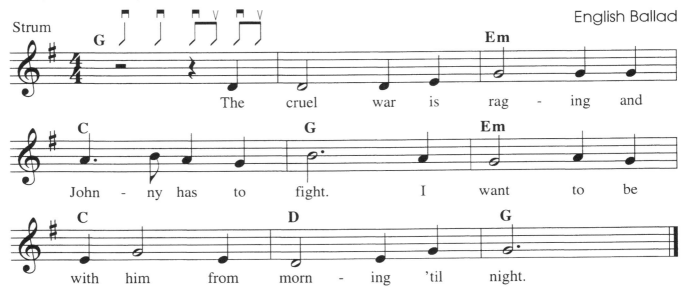

2. I'll go to your captain, get down upon my knees,
   Ten thousand gold guineas, I'd give for your release.

3. Ten thousand gold guineas, it grieves my heart so;
   Won't you let me go with you? Oh, no, my love, no.

4. Tomorrow is Sunday and Monday is the day,
   Your captain calls for you, and you must obey.

5. Your captain calls for you, it grieves my heart so,
   Won't you let me go with you? Oh, no, my love, no.

6. Your waist is too slender, your fingers are too small.
   Your cheeks are too rosy to face the cannonball.

7. Your cheeks are too rosy, it grieves my heart so.
   Won't you let me go with you? Oh, no, my love, no.

8. Johnny, oh Johnny, I think you are unkind.
   I love you far better than all other mankind.

9. I love you far better than tongue can express,
   Won't you let me go with you? Oh, yes, my love, yes.

10. I'll pull back my hair, men's clothes I'll put on,
    I'll pass for your comrade as we march along.

11. I'll pass for your comrade and none will ever guess,
    Won't you let me go with you? Yes, my love, yes.

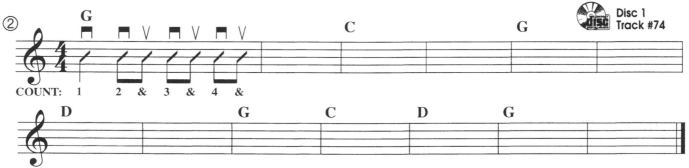

Ain't Gonna Rain No More

AMERICAN FOLK SONG

Disc 1 Track #75

Strum

Oh   what did the black-bird   say to the crow,   "It   ain't gon-na rain no more,   Ain't gon-na hail and it   ain't gon-na snow,   It   ain't gon-na rain no more."

CHORUS

Oh, it   ain't gon-na rain no   more, no more, It   ain't gon-na rain no   more.   How in the heck can I   wash my neck, when it   ain't gon-na rain no   more?

Verse 2:
G
Bake those biscuits good and brown,
D
It ain't gonna rain no more.

Swing your partner 'round and 'round,
G
It ain't gonna rain no more. *Chorus*

Verse 3:
G
It ain't gonna rain no more, no more,
D
It ain't gonna rain no more,

How do you suppose the old bird knows,
G
It ain't gonna rain no more. *Chorus*

Verse 4:
G
Thunder, lightning from the sky
D
It ain't gonna rain no more.

Saw Uncle Ezra floatin' by!
G
It ain't gonna rain no more? *Chorus*

Verse 5:
G
Pigs, cows, chickens and a goose!
D
It ain't gonna rain no more,

Whole darn barnyard's on the loose!
G
It ain't gonna rain no more! *Chorus*

Assignment: Make up your own verse to this song.

New Strum Patterns for 3/4 Time

Disc 1
Track #76

The following strum pattern will work well with songs written in 3/4 time.

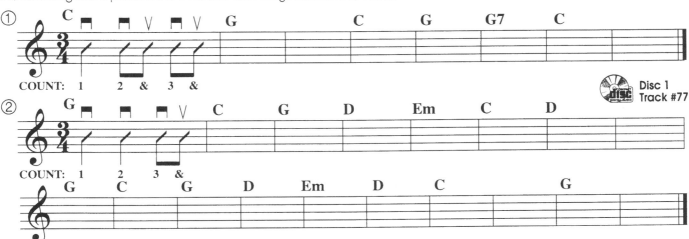

Play the following Mexican song using one of the strum patterns shown above.

Disc 1
Track #78

Las Mañanitas / Morning Greetings

(Birthday Song)

MEXICAN SONG

Si el sereno de la esquina
Me quisiera hacer favor,
De apagar su linternita
Mientras que pasa mi amor. *Chorus*

Amapolita morada
De los llanos de Tepic,
Si no estás enamorada,
Enamórate de mí. *Chorus*

Ahora sí señor sereno,
Le agradezco su favor;
Encienda su linternita,
Que ya ha pasado mi amor. *Chorus*

Oh lamplighter on the corner,
Please just listen to my song,
And blow out your little lantern
As my love passes along. *Chorus*

Little poppy, scarlet poppy,
On the meadows growing free,
If you're not in love with someone,
Please fall in love then with me. *Chorus*

Oh lamplighter, 1 do thank you
For the favor that you've done.
Now you can relight your lantern,
Because my love's come and gone. *Chorus*

Blues

Blues is an American music form. Its earliest forms were work songs and "field hollers" sung among the slaves. At first, blues was strictly a vocal music form, but gradually musicians of all types embraced the form. Traditional blues has 12 measures. Blues songs reflect times of troubles but often have a humorous twist.

Around 1900 a black band leader named W.C. Handy became popular and wrote such hits as "St. Louis Blues," "Beale Street Blues" and "Memphis Blues." Other early Blues artists included Blind Blake, Robert Johnson, Lonnie Johnson, and Louis Armstrong. Later band leaders like Count Basie and Duke Ellington, along with singers like Billie Holiday and Jimmy Rushing furthered the form. The modern blues era was ushered in by saxophonist Charlie Parker. Today blues is an essential part of all jazz and popular music. Who are some of today's famous blues' artists?

Midnight Special

Disc 1
Track #79

Prison Song

Wake up in the morn - in' when the ding dong rings

March up to the ta - ble, You see the same old things.

Let the Mid - night Spe - cial shine its light on me,

Let the Mid-night Spe - cial shine its ev-er lov-in' light on me.

Verse 1. Sister Sadie said she loved me, But she told a lie
'Cause she has not seen me- since last July.
She brought me coffee, she brought me tea,
She brought me lots of things, but not the jail house key. *Chorus*

> **Thought Question: What is the Midnight Special?**

Tab on Four Strings
Scarborough Fair

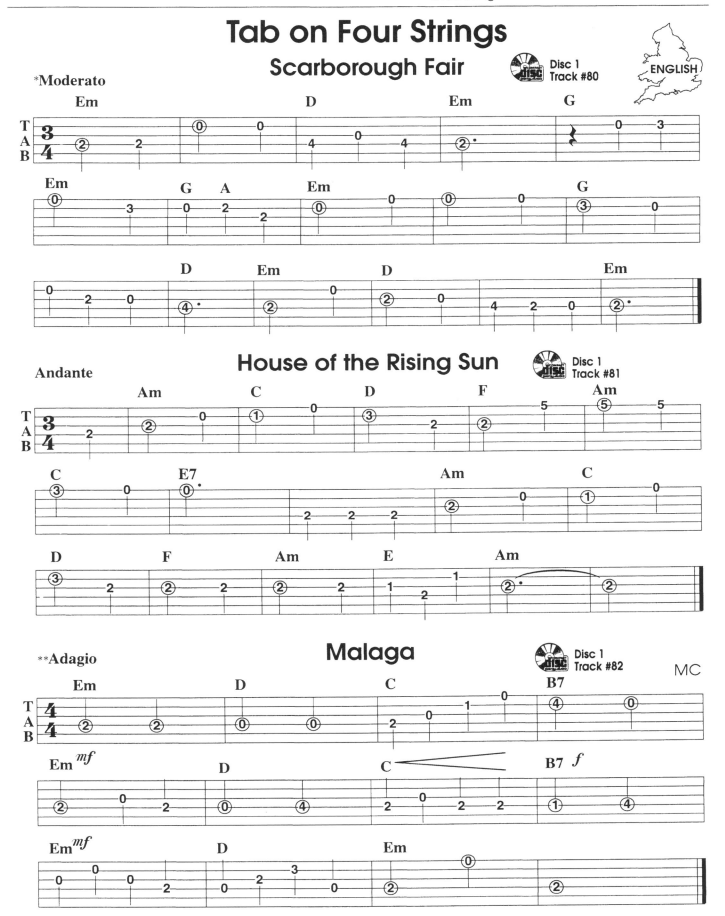

Moderato - medium speed (see p. 131)
**Adagio - slowly (see p. 131)*

Old Man and the Sea

Disc 1
Track #83

Arranged by
M. C.

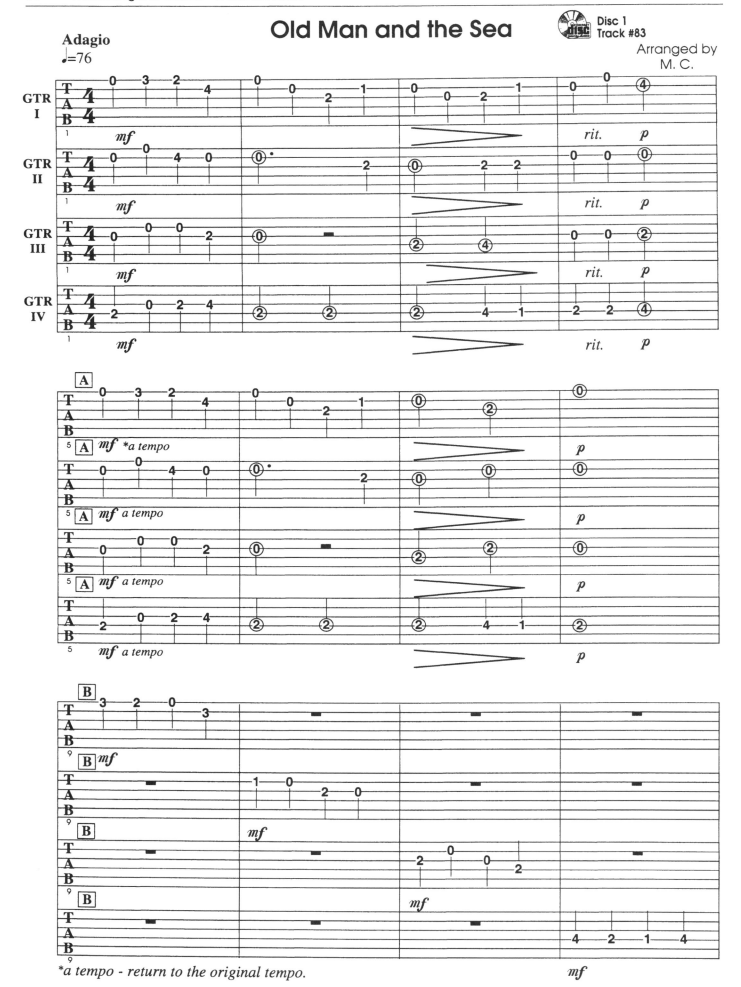

*a tempo - return to the original tempo.

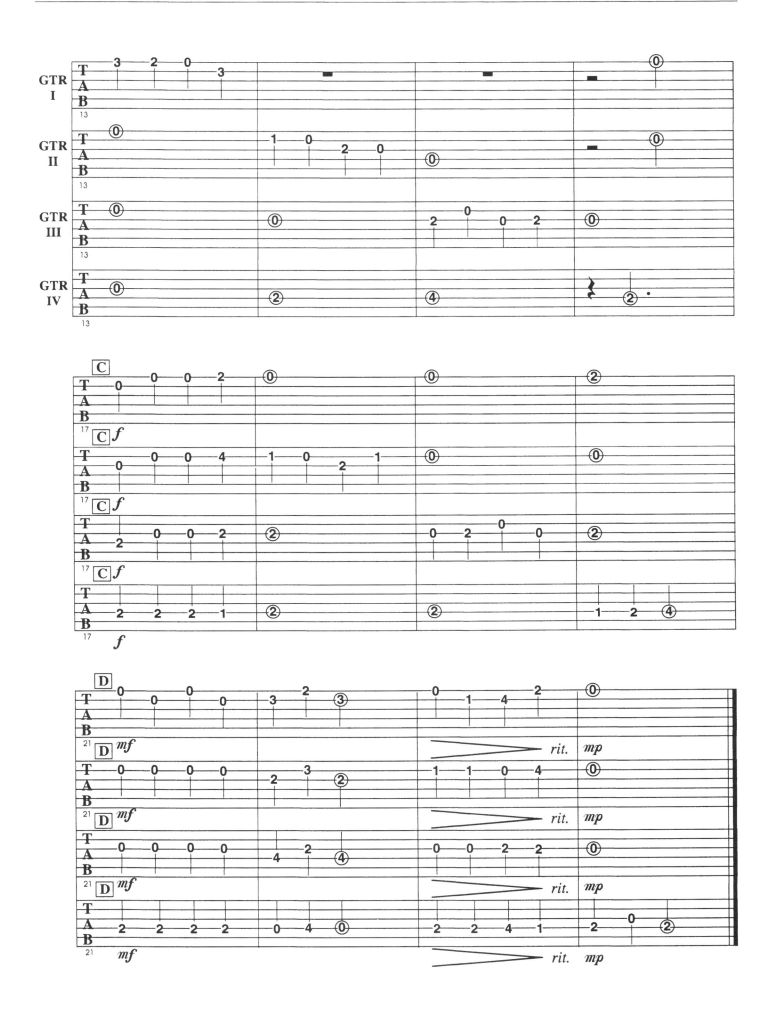

Notes on the 4th String

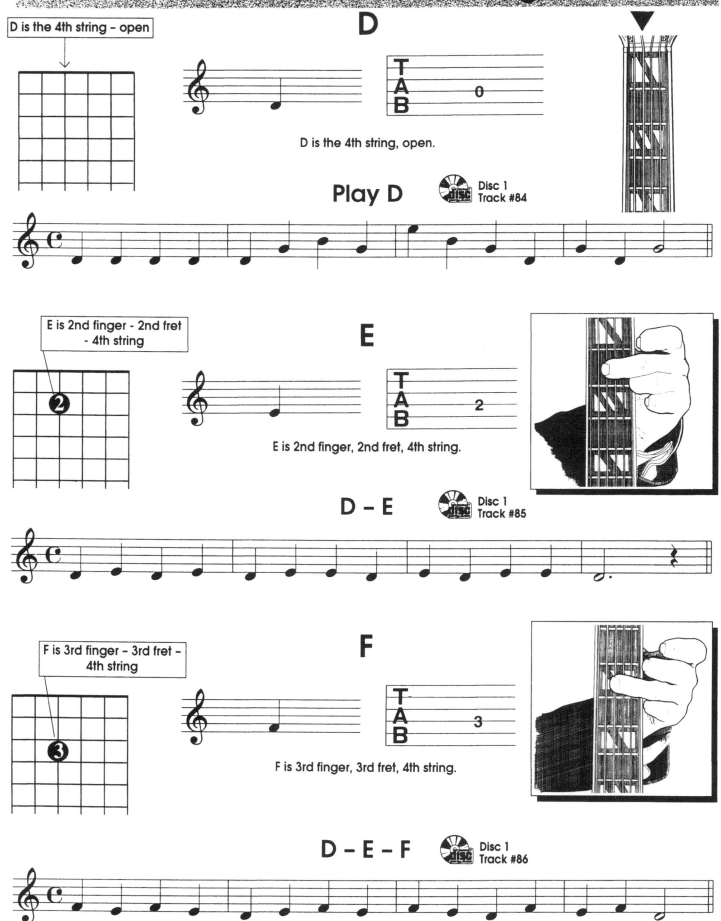

D

D is the 4th string – open

D is the 4th string, open.

Play D — Disc 1 Track #84

E

E is 2nd finger - 2nd fret - 4th string

E is 2nd finger, 2nd fret, 4th string.

D – E — Disc 1 Track #85

F

F is 3rd finger - 3rd fret - 4th string

F is 3rd finger, 3rd fret, 4th string.

D – E – F — Disc 1 Track #86

Morning Song

Disc 1
Track #87

EARLY AMERICAN
HYMN MELODY

Repeat Sign

Repeat signs look like this:

When they occur, repeat the music found between the signs.

Cripple Creek

Disc 1
Track #88

Western American
Gold Mining Song

Come With Me My Giselle

by Adam de la Halle

Disc 1
Track #89

13TH CENTURY ENGLISH

*Allegro - quickly (see p. 131)

The Guitar in Spain

The guitar has its roots in Spain. It appeared in Spain in the early sixteenth century. The first guitars had four sets of double strings called courses. Early guitars were used as solo and accompaniment instruments. As the modern guitar developed, double fifth and sixth strings were added. The single six-string guitar appeared in Spain around 1820. The change to single strings had been made earlier by the French in the 1770s. The Spanish probably chose to leave the strings double for a longer time because it made the guitar louder, which was better for accompanying Spanish dancing and singing done in a style of music called Flamenco. The Spanish guitar builder, Antonio de Torres, developed and standardized the classical guitar in the 1850s.

Spanish Nights

Disc 1
Track #90

Four-String Blues

Disc 1
Track #91

Number the Stars

Disc 1
Track #92

Parson's Farewell

Disc 1
Track #93

Medium Tempo

Acc. Chords

English Country Dance
John Playford - 1651

Na Pali Coast

Disc 1
Track #94

Moderato

Acc. Chords

Rounds on 4 Strings
Member of the Wedding

Disc 1
Track #95

Moderato

And Then There Were None

Disc 1
Track #96

Andante

Watership Down

Disc 1
Track #97

Allegro

Charlotte's Web

Disc 1
Track #98

Arranged by
M. C.

Am   Learn the two new chords drawn here.   D7   Disc 1 Track #99

Practice the following exercises and songs which contain **Am** and **D7**. In each measure, play the strum pattern which is written in the first measure.

Molly Malone

Disc 2 Track #1

In   Dub - lin's fair   cit - y   where   girls   are   so   pret - ty,   oh,

there's   where   I   met   my   sweet   Mol - ly   Ma - lone,   And she

Wheeled   her   wheel - bar - row   through the   streets   broad   and   nar - row   cry - ing

"Cock - les   and   mus - sels,   A - live,   a - live - o."   "A

live,   a - live - o,   a - live,   a - live - o"   Cry - ing

"Cock - les   and   mus - sels,   A - live,   a - live - o."

A7 and E7 Chords

The fingerings for **A7** and **E7** chords are shown on the diagrams below. Notice there are two fingerings for each chord. One is not necessarily better than the other and either fingering may be used. The first forms are easier. Eventually, both forms of each chord should be learned.

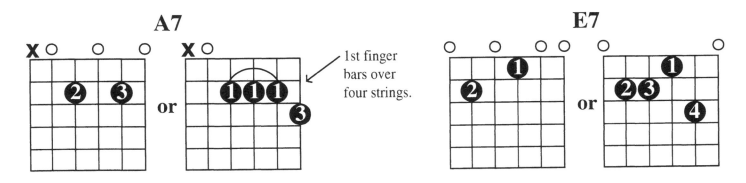

Practice the following exercises which contain A7 and/or E7.

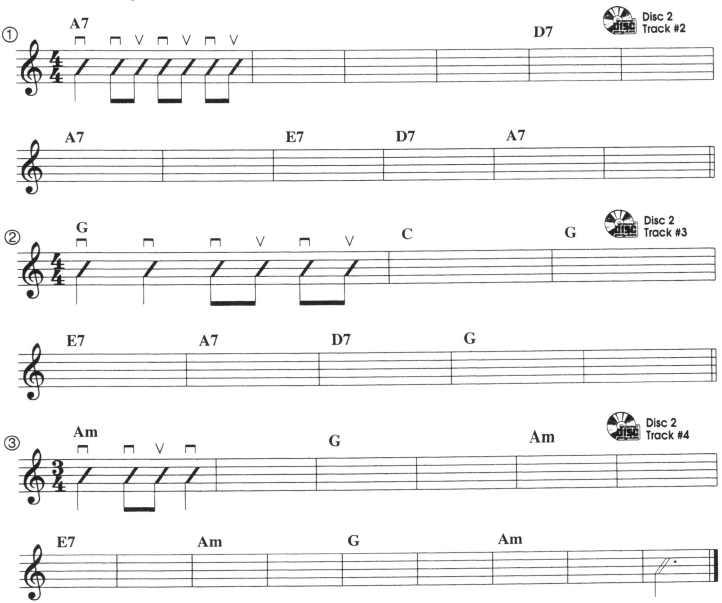

My Bonnie Lies Over the Ocean

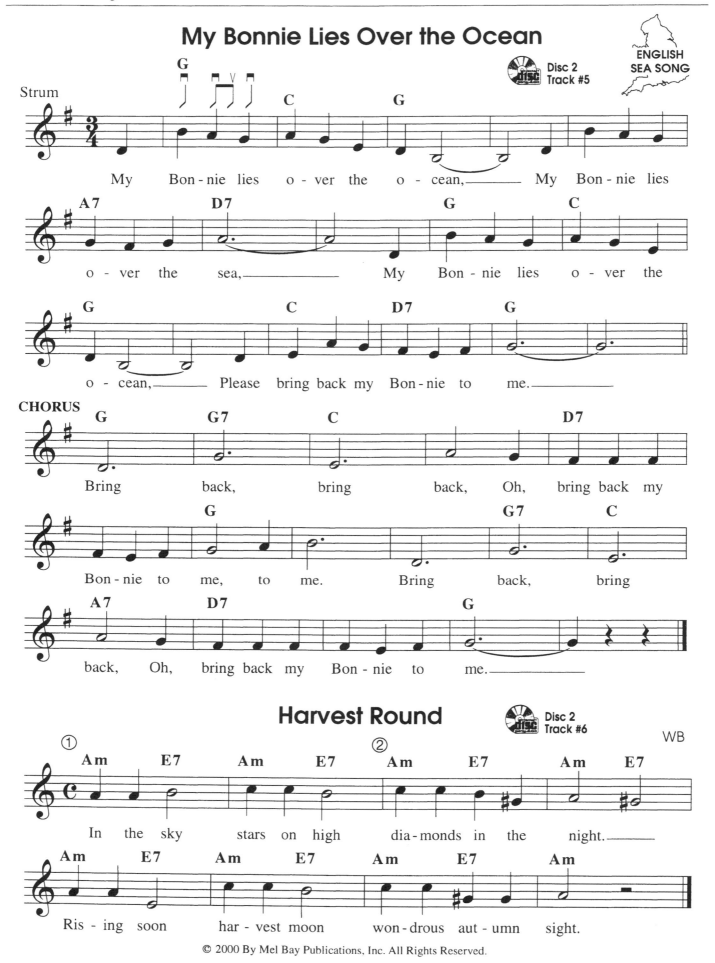

Disc 2 Track #5

ENGLISH SEA SONG

B7 and Bm Chords

Learn the **B7** and **Bm** chords drawn below and practice the exercises containing these chords. As with the other exercises in this book, use the same strum pattern which is written in the first measure to play the other measures.

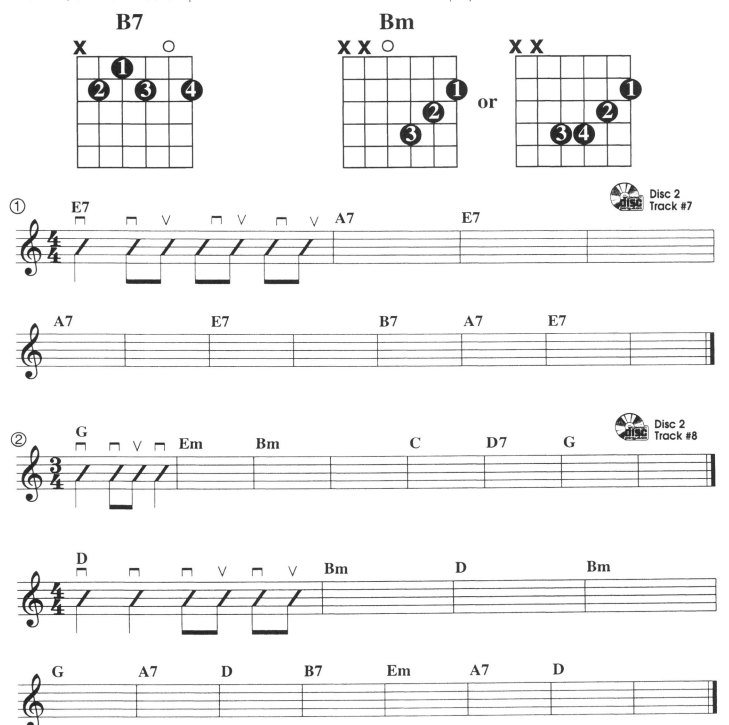

Disc 2
Track #10

Land of the Silver Birch

Canadian Indian

Strum

Em · · · · Am

Land of the sil-ver birch, home of the bea-ver, And where the

Em   B7   CHORUS Em

might-y moose wan-ders at will.   Blue lakes and rock-y shores,

B7   Em   D   Em

I will re-turn once more, Land   of   my   peo-

C   D   Em

ple,   Land   of   my   peo -   ple.

Em
2. High on a rocky ledge I'll build my wigwam,
Am   **Em**   **B7**
Close by the water's edge silent and still. *Chorus*

Em
3. Down in the forest glade deep in the lowlands,
Am   **Em**   **B7**
My heart cries out for thee, Hills of the North. *Chorus*

Vocabulary: aspen, corpse, briar.

Barbara Allen

Disc 2
Track #11

Strum

D   Bm   G   D

Late in the sea-son of the year, the yel-low leaves are fall-ing.___

G   D   G   D

Sweet Will-iam he___ was tak-en sick for the love of Bar-b'ry Al-len.___

2. He sent his servant to the town,
The town where she was dwelling.
Rise you up to your master's call
If your name be Barbara Al-len.

3. 'Twas in the merry month of May.
When green buds, they were swellin',
Sweet William on his deathbed lay
For the love of Barb'ry Allen

4. He sent his servant to the town
Where Barb'ry was a dwellin',
"My master's sick and bids you come,
If your name be Barb'ry Allen."

5. So slowly, slowly got she up,
And slowly she came nigh him,
And all she said when she got there,
"Young man, I think your dyin'."

6. "Oh, yes, I'm sick and very sick,
For death is in me dwellin'.
No better can I ever be,
If can't have Barb'ry Allen."

7. Then lightly tripped she down the stairs,
He trembled like an aspen,
"'Tis vain, 'tis vain, my dear young man,
To pine for Barb'ry Allen."

8. He turned his pale face to the wall,
For death was in him dwellin',
"Adieu, adieu, my friends all 'round,
Be kind to Barb'ry Allen."

9. As she went down the long piney walk,
The birds, they kept a-singin',
They sang so clear, they seemed to say,
"Hard-hearted Barb'ry Allen."

10. She looked to the east, she looked to the west,
She spied his corpse a-comin',
"Lay down, lay down that deathly frame
That I may look upon him."

11. The more she looked, the more she wept
Till she burst out a-crying;
"Oh take from me this very young man,
I think that I am dying."

12. They took him to the new churchyard,
And that is where they laid him.
They buried his lover by his side,
Her name-was Barbara Allen.

13. Out of his grave there sprang a rose,
And our of hers a briar
They grew and tied a true lover's knot,
The rose around the briar.

Cinq

Disc 2
Track #12

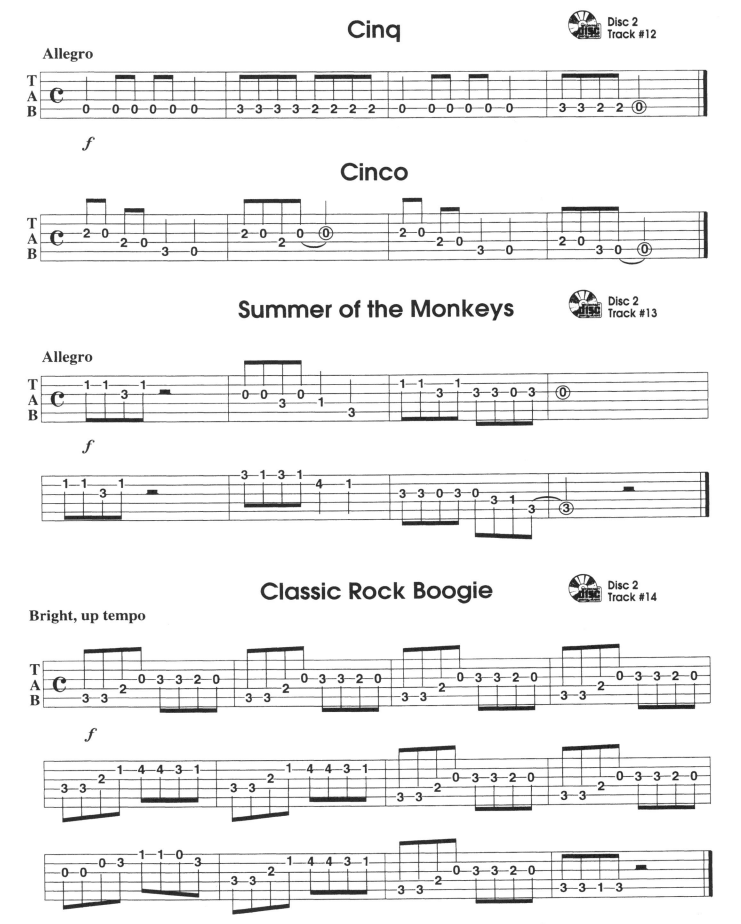

Cinco

Summer of the Monkeys

Disc 2
Track #13

Classic Rock Boogie

Disc 2
Track #14

Notes on the 5th String

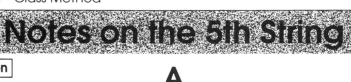

A is the 5th string - open

A

A is the 5th string, open.

Disc 2 Track #15

Play A

B is 2nd finger - 2nd fret - 5th string

B

B is 2nd finger, 2nd fret, 5th string.

Acc. Chords

Am   G   Am   G   Am G Am G   Am G Am

C

C is 3rd finger, 3rd fret, 5th string.

Disc 2 Track #16

Maniac Magee

Acc. Chords

Am   E7   Am

E7   Am   E7   Am

Disc 2 Track #17

A String Study #1

Acc. Chords

Am   C   G   Am   C   G   Am

Duet

Disc 2
Track #18

A, Andre
1714-1799

Moderato

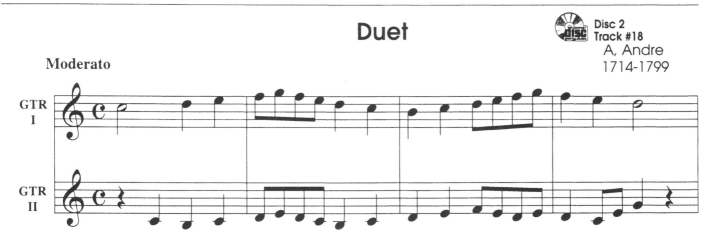

Johann Sebastian Bach

Bach

Johann Sebastian Bach lived from 1685 to 1750. He was a German composer and a master of the period known as the Baroque Period in music. He spent most of his life as a church organist and wrote many compositions for organ. He also wrote compositions for orchestra and choral pieces known as chorales and cantatas. He is considered the "master of the fugue" (the fugue is a type of musical composition prevalent during the Baroque Period in which the beginning melody is repeated and played in various forms throughout the piece).

GERMANY

Jesu, Joy of Man's Desiring

Disc 2
Track #19

Adagio

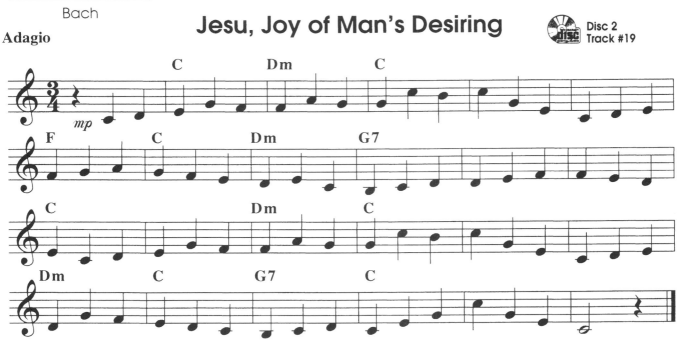

First and Second Endings

Sometimes in a song a first and second ending appear (⌐1.⌐   ⌐2.⌐). When this occurs, take the first ending and observe the repeat signs. Then, on the second time through, skip the first ending, play the second ending and continue with the music. (Sometimes the song will end with the second ending.)

Johannes Brahms

Johannes Brahms was a German composer of the Romantic Period. He lived from 1833-1897. Brahms was an excellent pianist and wrote many fine works for piano. He also wrote every type of music except opera. He is known especially for his symphonies.

Hungarian Dance #4

The Sally Gardens

*ff fortissimo - very loud (see p. 131)

Rounds on 5 Strings

Si Cantemo

Disc 2
Track #22

The Picking School

Disc 2
Track #23

Dotted Quarter Note

A dotted quarter note receives one-and-a-half counts

is the same as

Count: 1   &   2   1   &   2

Compare the rhythm and note values

1 & 2 & 1 & 2 & 1 & 2 & 1 & 2 & 1 & 2 & 1 & 2 &

Study

Disc 2 Track #24

Dotted quarter note

Count: 1 & 2 & 3 & 4 &

Moderately
Acc. Chords

Across Five Aprils

Disc 2 Track #25

Am   C   Am   C   Am   C   E7

Am   C   Em   Am   Em   Am

Slowly
Acc. Chords

Call the Ewes

Disc 2 Track #26

SCOTTISH BALLAD

Dm   C   Am   G

Am   C   Dm   C   Am

Andante

Cumberland Ridge

Disc 2 Track #27

Am   C   Am   C   Am   C   Esus   E7

Am   C   Am   C   Am   E7   Am

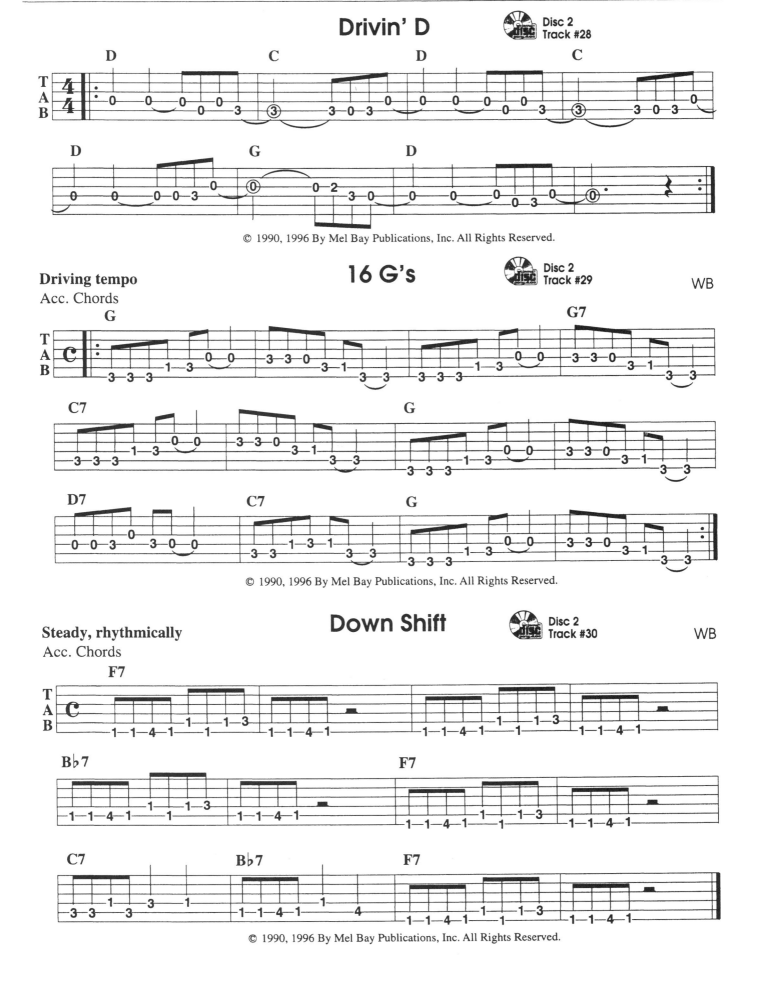

Drivin' D

Disc 2 Track #28

16 G's

Disc 2 Track #29

WB

Driving tempo
Acc. Chords

Down Shift

Disc 2 Track #30

WB

Steady, rhythmically
Acc. Chords

Notes on the 6th String

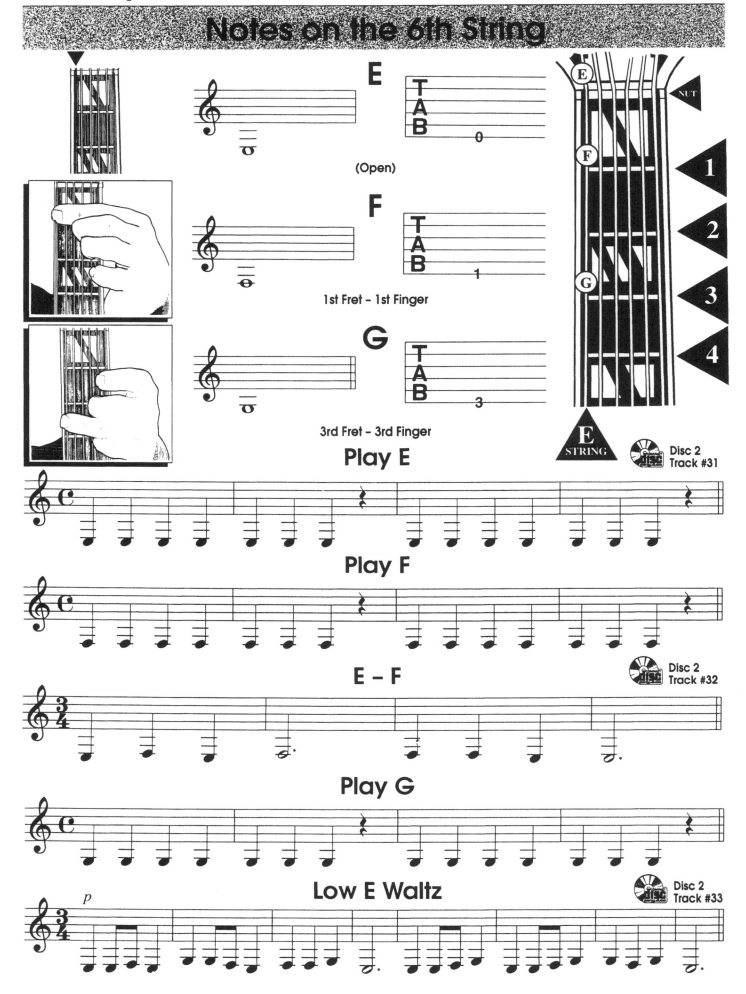

E

(Open)

F

1st Fret – 1st Finger

G

3rd Fret – 3rd Finger

Disc 2
Track #31

Play E

Play F

Disc 2
Track #32

E – F

Play G

Low E Waltz

Disc 2
Track #33

Blow Away the Morning Dew

Brightly
Acc. Chords

Disc 2
Track #34
Sea Chanty

Introducing the A Note

A

5th Fret
4th Finger

E STRING

Disc 2
Track #35

Blow, Ye Winds

Disc 2
Track #36

Brightly
Acc. Chords

Sea Chanty

Early American Hymn

Disc 2
Track #37

Acc. Chords

Star of the County Down
Guitar Ensemble

Disc 2
Track #38

Arranged by
M. C.

IRISH BALLAD

A Review of the Basic Notes
Insert the Alphabet Letters, Fret Numbers and String Number

The C Scale

C Scale

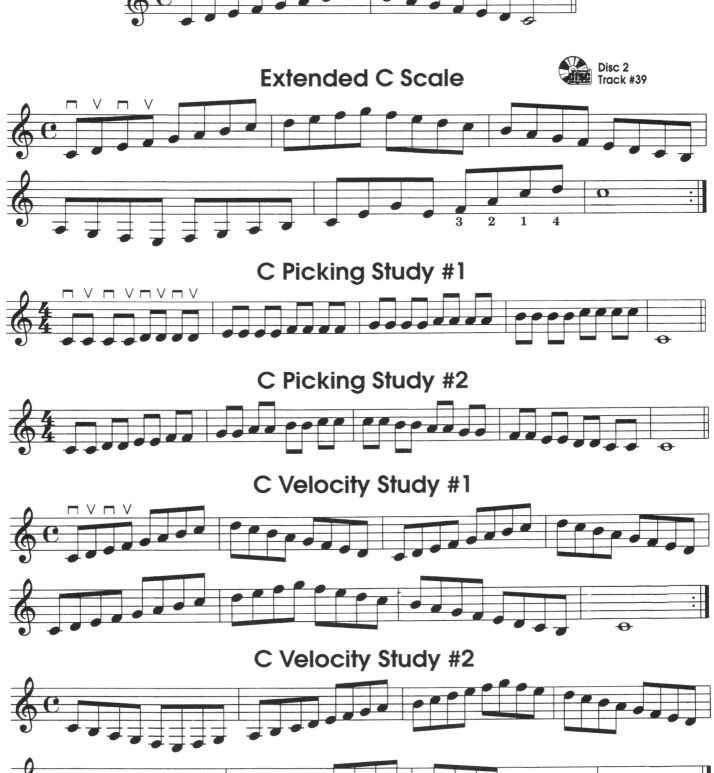

Extended C Scale

Disc 2
Track #39

C Picking Study #1

C Picking Study #2

C Velocity Study #1

C Velocity Study #2

New Chords

Study

Disc 2 Track #40

I Ride an Old Paint

Cowboy Song

Disc 2 Track #41

Strum

I ride an old paint,— I lead an old dan,— I'm goin' to Mon-

tan - a to throw the Hou - li - han. They feed in the cou - lees, they

wa - ter in the draw, Their tails are all mat - ted, their backs are all raw.

Ride a - round, lit - tle do - gies, ride a - round___ them___

slow. For the fier - y and snuf - fy are rar - in' to go.

2. Old Bill Jones had two daughters and a song,
One went to Denver the other went wrong.
His wife got killed in a pool-room fight,
But still he keeps singing from morning till night. *Chorus*

3. I've worked in the city, worked on the farm,
And all I've got to show is the muscle in my arm.
Patches on my pants, callous on my hand
And I'm goin' to Montana to throw the houlihan. *Chorus*

4. Oh, when I die, take my saddle from the wall,
Put it on my pony and lead him from the stall.
Tie my bones to his back, turn our faces to the west,
And we'll ride the prairies we love the best.

Jargan	
old paint	draw
old dan	dogies
houlihan	rarin' to go
coulees	goin'

Pay Me My Money Down

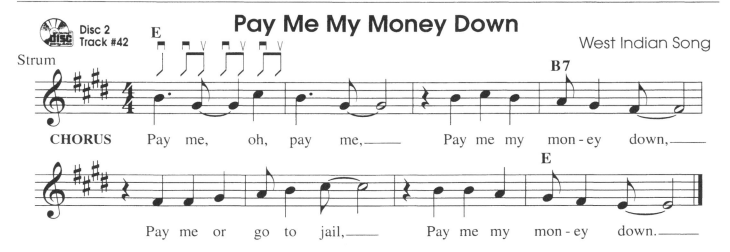

West Indian Song

CHORUS Pay me, oh, pay me,___ Pay me my mon-ey down,___

Pay me or go to jail,___ Pay me my mon-ey down.___

I thought I heard the captain say,
Pay me my money down.
Tomorrow is our sailing day.
Pay me my money down. *Chorus*

My Home Across the Smoky Mountains

My home's a - cross the Smok-y Moun - tains, My home's a -

cross the Smok-y Moun - tains, My home's a - cross the Smok-y

Moun - tains, And I'll nev-er get to see you an-y more, more,

more, ___ And I'll nev-er get to see you an-y more___

2. Good-bye, honey, sugar darling (3)
And I'll never get to see you any more, more, more,
And I'll never get to see you any more.

3. Rock my honey, feed her candy (3)
And I'll never get to see you any more, more, more,
And I'll never get to see you any more.

4. I'm going back to the red clay country, (3)
And I'll never get to see you any more, more, more,
And I'll never get to see you any more.

Playing Two Chords Per Measure

Often a song will have more than one chord per measure. This requires changing chords quickly. The following songs have some measures containing several different chords. Can you find those measures? For now, if two chords appear in a measure, do not divide the strum pattern. Divide the measure and use only down strums. Then, return to the strum pattern if there is one chord in the measure.

Peace Like a River

Disc 2
Track #44

Lively tempo

Spiritual

I've got peace like a ri-ver, I've got peace like a ri-ver, I've got

peace like a ri-ver in my soul; I've got peace like a ri-ver, I've got

peace like a ri-ver, I've got peace like a ri-ver in my soul.

2. Joy like a fountain.   3. Love like an ocean.

Scotland's Burning
(4 Part Round)

Disc 2
Track #45

SCOTLAND

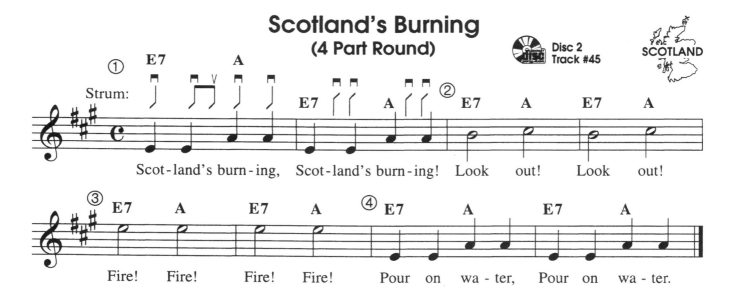

Scot-land's burn-ing, Scot-land's burn-ing! Look out! Look out!

Fire! Fire! Fire! Fire! Pour on wa-ter, Pour on wa-ter.

America the Beautiful

Katherine Lee Bates

AMERICAN SONG

Disc 2 Track #46

Oh beau-ti-ful for spa-cious skies, For am-ber waves of grain, For pur-ple moun-tain maj-es-ties, A-bove the fruit-ed plain! A-mer-i-ca! A-mer-i-ca! God shed His grace on thee, And crown thy good with broth-er-hood From sea to shin-ing sea.

2. O beautiful for pilgrim feet, Whose stern, impassioned stress,
A thorough fare for freedom beat, Across the wilderness!
America! America! God mend thine every flaw,
Confirm thy soul in self control, Thy liberty in law.

3. O beautiful for heroes proved in liberating strife,
Who more than self their country loved, And mercy more than life!
America! America! May God thy gold refine,
Till all success be nobleness, And every gain divine.

4. O beautiful for patriot dream, That sees beyond the years,
Thine alabaster cities gleam, Undimmed by human tears!
America! America! God shed his grace on thee,
And crown thy good with brotherhood From sea to shining sea.

America

Disc 2 Track #47

Henry Carey

My coun-try 'tis of thee, sweet land of lib-er-ty, Of thee I sing. Land where my fa-thers died! Land of the Pil-grim's pride! From ev-'ry moun-tain-side Let free-dom ring!

2. My native country, thee, Land of the noble free,
Thy name I love: I love thy rocks and rills, Thy woods and
Templed hills; My heart with rapture thrills Like that above.

3. Let music swell the breeze, And ring from all the trees
Sweet freedom's song: Let mortal tongues awake; Let all that
Breathe partake; Let rocks their silence break, The sound prolong.

4. Our fathers' God, to Thee, Author of liberty,
To Thee we sing: Long may our land be bright With freedom's
Holy light; Protect us by Thy might, Great God, our King!

Sharps

A "**sharp**" (♯) placed in front of a note raises the pitch 1/2 step or 1 fret. Study the notes below. We will learn more about sharps as we learn specific keys later on.

1st String

When a note is sharped, all notes of that pitch remain sharped throughout the measure unless a **natural sign** (♮) appears. A natural sign cancels a sharp. At the end of the measure, the sharp is cancelled.

1st String Sharps and Naturals

2nd String

3rd String

4th String

5th String

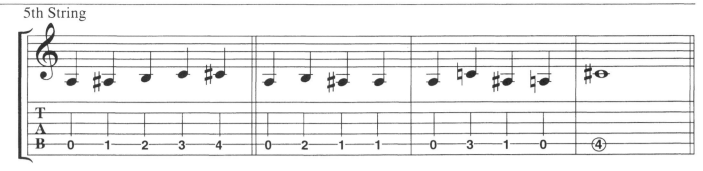

6th String

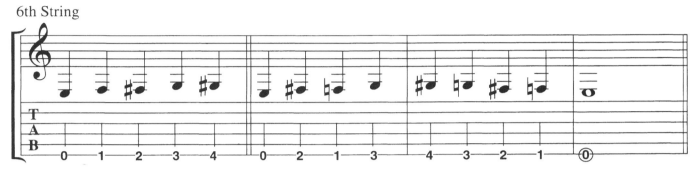

Walking Guitar

Disc 2
Track #48

WB

Andante

Quiz

Grade _____

Insert Correct Note Name, Fret Number and String

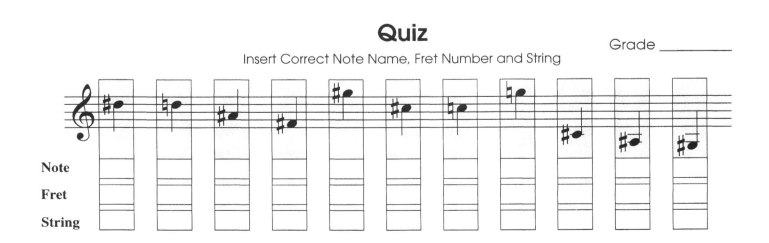

Note

Fret

String

William Billings (1746 - 1800)

William Billings was an early American composer who had a strong influence on the development of church music in the United States. He wrote the first published collection of music which was completely American. Billings had little formal education and attended singing schools in Boston. He had one leg, one eye, and one slightly withered arm. Despite his physical handicaps, Billings was a successful singing teacher and wrote over 340 compositions, most of which were psalm and hymn tunes. He lived quite comfortably and made his living teaching and composing until the late 1780s when, because of financial trouble, he had to work for a time as a sealer of leather. A benefit concert was even given to help raise money for him. Billings' later works made him little money, and towards the end of his life, he worked teaching in schools near Boston.

Morpheus
(from "Music in Miniatures," 1779)

Disc 2
Track #49

Written 3 years after the signing of
the Declaration of Independence

William Billings
1746-1800
Arranged by M. C.

Greensleeves

Disc 2
Track #50

OLD ENGLISH

Moderately slow
Acc. Chords

French Carol

Disc 2
Track #51

FRANCE

Adagio

Edvard Grieg

Edvard Grieg was a Norwegian composer who lived during the Romantic Period. He was born in 1843 and died in 1907. Much of his music was built upon and captured the melodic and rhythmic elements of Norwegian folk music; and thus, is considered "nationalistic."

NORWAY

Anitra's Dance Theme

Disc 2
Track #52

Edvard Grieg

Flowing, dance like

Greensleeves
Guitar Ensemble

Disc 2
Track #53

Arranged by
M. C.

Key Signature

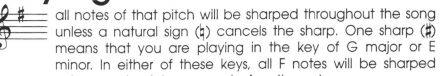

When a sharp appears here all notes of that pitch will be sharped throughout the song unless a natural sign (♮) cancels the sharp. One sharp (♯) means that you are playing in the key of G major or E minor. In either of these keys, all F notes will be sharped unless a natural sign occurs before the note.

Study

Disc 2 Track #56

O Come, O Come Emmanuel

ENGLISH CAROL

Slowly

Call of the Wild

Moderato   Disc 2 Track #57

Disc 2 Track #58

Johnny Has Gone for a Soldier

EARLY AMERICAN BALLAD

This is a beautiful Irish melody which was altered. It was sung during the *Revolutionary War* by early American colonists.

*Largo

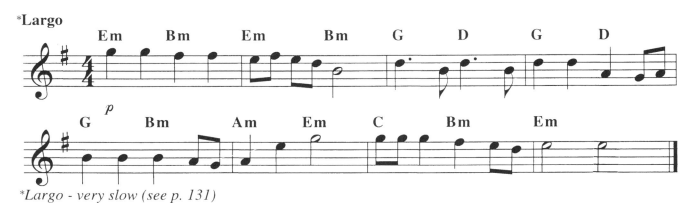

*Largo - very slow (see p. 131)

The Cay
(Reggae Ensemble)

Disc 2
Track #59

(A "cay" is an uninhabited island)

Arranged by
M. C.

A fifth guitar part may be added by strumming the chords using this pattern in each measure. See p. 120 for the fingering of the F chord.

Russian Folk Song

Disc 2 Track #60

Moderato

RUSSIA

Shabat Shalom
(Song for the Sabbath)

Disc 2 Track #61

ISRAELI SONG

Andante

Section A

Section B

(Go back and play Section A
once more to end the piece)

The Blues Progression

One of the most popular forms of the blues is the 12-bar blues progression. The term **progression** refers to a series of chords. **Twelve-bar** means the progression is 12 measures long. *The three chords used in the basic 12-bar progression are the I, IV, and V chords.* The **I chord** (sometimes called the **tonic**) has the same letter name as the key in which you are playing. For example, the I chord in the key of C is C. The **IV chord (subdominant)** has the letter name which is four steps up the major scale from the I chord. The IV chord in the key of C is F. The **V chord (dominant)** has the same letter name as the fifth step up the major scale from the I chord. The V chord in the key of C is G. The following chart shows the I, IV, and V chords in the different keys. The most popular guitar keys are shown below. In the blues 7th chords are frequently used.

I (Tonic)	IV (Subdominant)	V (Dominant)
E (7)	A (7)	B (7)
A (7)	D (7)	E (7)
D (7)	G (7)	A (7)
G (7)	C (7)	D (7)

The formula for building the basic 12-bar blues progression is: four measures of the I chord, two measures of the IV chord, two measures of the I chord, one measure of the V chord, one measure of the IV chord, and two measures of the I chord. It's very common to replace the last measure of the I chord with a V chord if the progression is going to be repeated. This last measure is sometimes called the **turnaround.** The advantage of knowing the Roman numeral formula is that, by plugging in the correct I, IV, and V chords, you can play the blues in any key.

The following exercise is the basic 12-bar blues progression. Notice that the number of measures that each chord is played fits the blues formula. The chords in parentheses are the chords which would be used to play the blues in the key of E. Seventh chords (7) are commonly used on every chord in the blues because of their dissonant quality.

Play the following progression strumming down four times in each measure. While it may seem overly simple, strumming down four times in a measure was, and is, a fairly popular technique. Accent beats two and four.

Accent marks. Play the strums which have these marks above them louder.

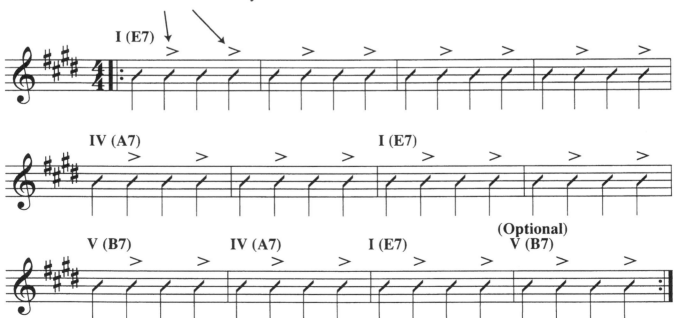

The next progression is a very **common variation of the 12-bar blues**. The IV chord has been added in the second measure. Remember, the V chord in the last measure is optional. This chord can be played if the progression is going to be repeated. When not repeating the progression, play the I chord in the last measure. Practice strumming this exercise. In each measure of the progression, play the strum pattern which is written in the first measure, This strum pattern works well when playing songs in 4/4.

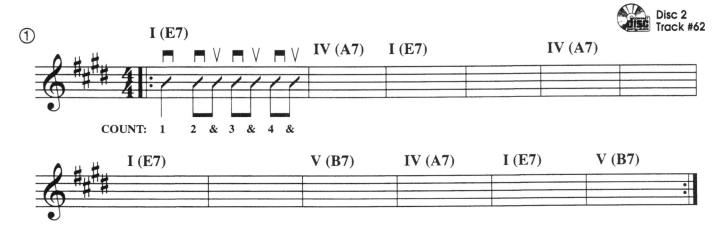

Strum the next progression which is a **blues in the key of A**. In each measure, use the strum pattern which is written in the first measure. This is another strum pattern which works to accompany songs in 4/4.

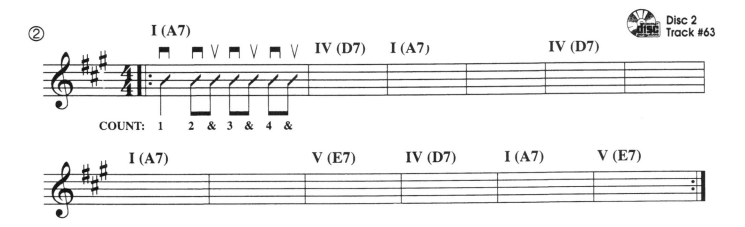

To play the blues in a minor key, the i and iv chords are minor and the V chord is still a seventh chord. Small Roman numerals indicate minor chords. Practice strumming the following blues in A minor. Use any of the strum patterns for 4/4. Remember to use the same strum pattern in each measure,

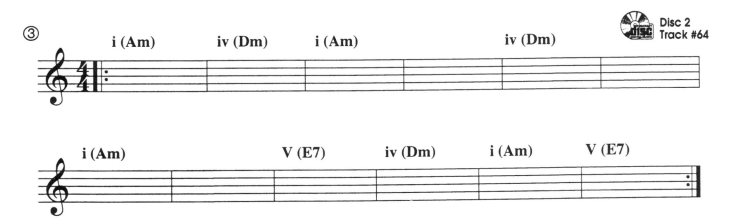

Practice strumming the following **blues songs**. Notice each song uses the 12-bar blues progression.

Baby Don't Love Me

Writing Blues Lyrics

Writing lyrics to a blues song can be very simple. All that is required is to rhyme one word. The common blues progression is twelve measures long. This 12-measure progression can be divided into three groups of four measures. Each group of four measures is called a *phrase*. Phrases are separated by pauses in the melody.

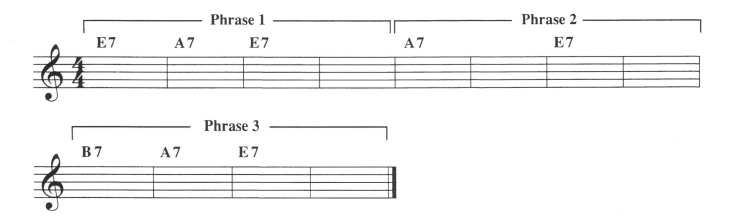

After each phrase there is usually a pause. Within each phrase, one or two sentences of lyrics can be written. For example:

In the blues, it is very common for the lyrics and the melody in the second phrase to be the same as the lyrics and melody in the first phrase.

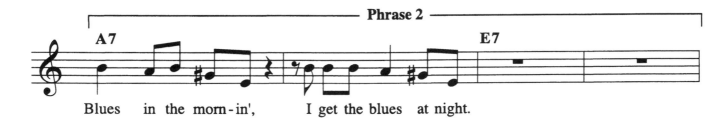

In the third phrase the lyrics and the melody usually change and the last word of the third phrase rhymes with the last word in phrases 1 and 2.

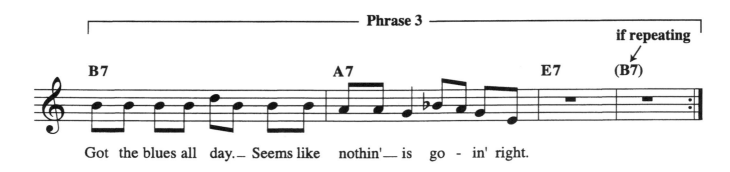

Written below is a 12-bar blues melody. Write in your own lyrics under the notes. You may have to modify the rhythm of the melody slightly to fit your words.

Writing Your Own Blues Song

Write your own lyrics to this blues melody.

_____ **Blues**

by _____

Lyrics: _____

_____

_____

Power Chords

The type of chord which is commonly used in rock and blues guitar playing is called a **power chord.** Power chords are written with the 5 next to the chord name (A5). Power chords may also be used when the written chord is a seventh (7) chord. The following diagrams show the A5, D5, and E5 chords. Only two strings are played on each chord. One of the strings played is open. Play the strings quickly so they sound simultaneously. The tablature and notes which are played are written next to each diagram. Hold each chord and play it several times.

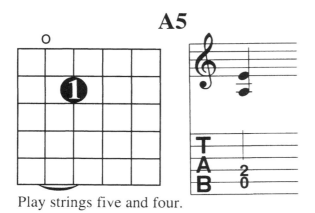

A5

Play strings five and four.

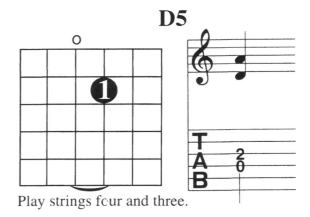

D5

Play strings four and three.

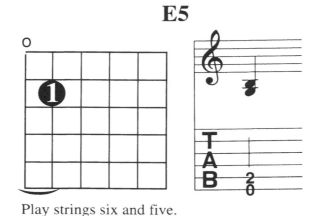

E5

Play strings six and five.

A popular way of using power chords for the guitar accompaniment is to play each chord eight times in a measure (two times to each beat). Play the next blues progression which shows how this is done. The eighth note strums are written as two strum bars connected with a beam ( ). This shows that the chord is played two times to each beat (once on the downbeat and once in between the beats). Notice that only downstrokes are used. Be sure to play only two strings on each power chord.

**Disc 2
Track #66**

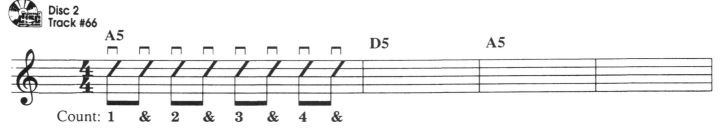

Count: 1   &   2   &   3   &   4   &

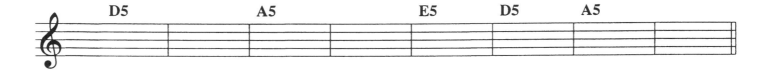

It is very common to play eighth notes (two notes or strums to a beat) to use **shuffle** or **swing** rhythm. This means that, rather than dividing the beat into two equal parts, the beat is divided into a long–short pattern. This gives the music a kind of bouncy feel. If you have a difficult time getting the swing feel, try thinking of the rhythm used in the *Battle Hymn of the Republic*. This song is usually sung with a swing rhythm.

Practice the last exercise again using swing (or shuffle) rhythm.

A common variation on the power chord involves adding a finger on the third, fourth, seventh, and eighth downstrokes of the measure. For example, on the A5 chord, play strings 5 and 4 together four times. Use only downstrokes. On the third and fourth strokes, add the left-hand third finger where the "X" is drawn on the diagram below. Do this twice in each measure. Be sure to leave the first finger down even when the third finger is added.

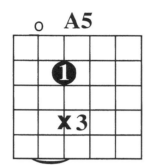

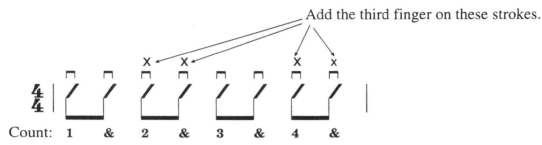

Add the third finger on these strokes.

The following shows the notation and tablature for this technique.

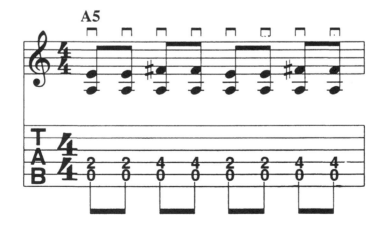

This technique could be used on the D5 chord by adding the third finger on the third string where the "X" is drawn.

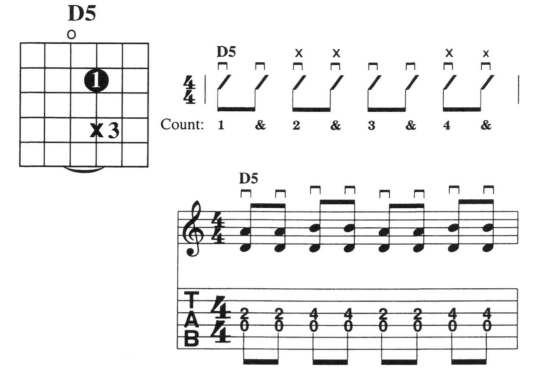

For the E5, add the third finger in the fourth fret on the fifth string.

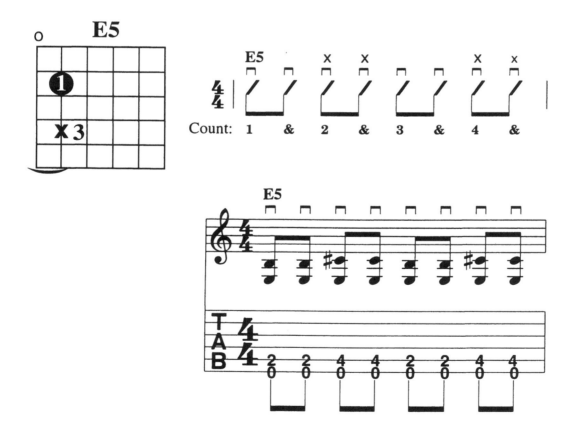

The next exercise uses this **variation on the power chords.**

Smithfield Boogie

Disc 2
Track #67

MC

Another popular variation on power chords is to add the left-hand third finger on the third and seventh downstrokes of the measure (beats two and four). In the next song, the guitar accompaniment uses this variation on the power chords. The melody is written on the top staff and the guitar part is written below. Remember, power chords can be used if the written chord is a seventh (7) chord.

Good Mornin' Blues

Disc 2
Track #68

Blues Quiz

Grade _____

1. How many measures are normally found in a blues progression? _____

2. What are the chords for blues in A? _____ _____ _____

3. Write the blues progression the key of E.

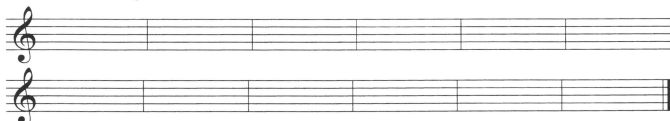

Flats and Natural Signs

A "**flat**" (♭) placed in front of a note *lowers* the pitch 1/2 step or 1 fret. Study the notes below. A **natural sign** (♮) cancels out a flat or sharp.

Accidentals

Sharp (♯), **flat** (♭), and **natural** (♮) **signs** are called *accidentals*. When an accidental appears in front of a note, it not only affects that note, but also the remaining notes in the measure which have the same pitch. At the end of the measure, the accidental is cancelled.

1st String

2nd String

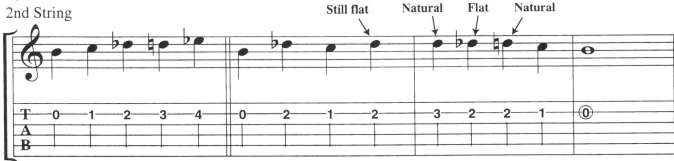

3rd String

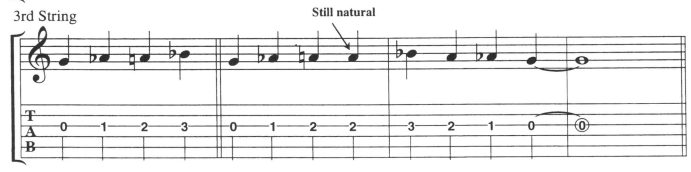

4th String

5th String

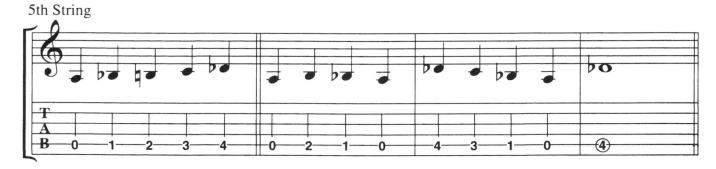

6th String

Benny's Flat

Flatpicking Solo

Allegro

Disc 2
Track #69

WB

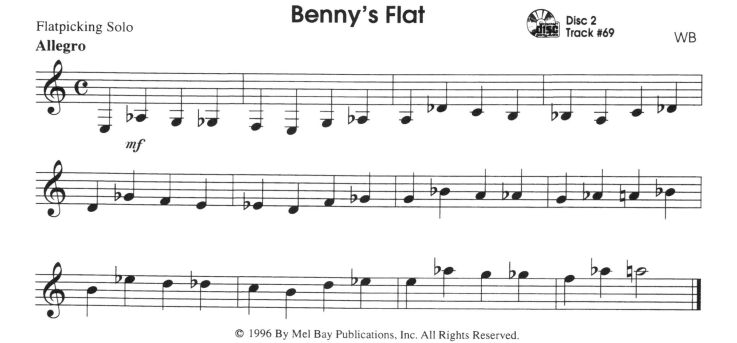

Key Signature - One Flat

When there is one flat in the key signature, the piece is in the key of F major or D minor. If one flat is in the key signature, flat all of the Bs throughout the piece, unless a natural sign is written.

Sakura

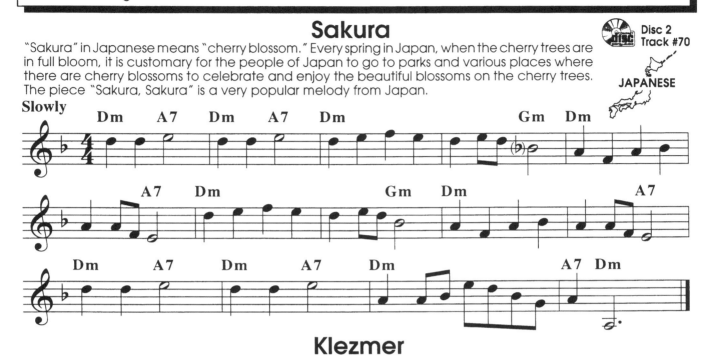

"Sakura" in Japanese means "cherry blossom." Every spring in Japan, when the cherry trees are in full bloom, it is customary for the people of Japan to go to parks and various places where there are cherry blossoms to celebrate and enjoy the beautiful blossoms on the cherry trees. The piece "Sakura, Sakura" is a very popular melody from Japan.

Disc 2
Track #70

JAPANESE

Klezmer

Klezmer is a Jewish folk music style. The word Klezmer comes from the Jewish words Kley zemer which means "vessels of song." It is the traditional instrumental music of the Jews. Klezmer began in the sixteenth century in Eastern Europe. Klezmer was the music traditionally played at Jewish weddings and other festive events. This style of music was originally used to accompany dances. The violin was the lead instrument playing the melody. Between 1800 and 1920, during the Jewish migration, when Klezmer music came to America, the clarinet replaced the violin as the dominant instrument.

The following piece is an example of Klezmer music.

Terk in America

Disc 2
Track #71

Klezmer

Bridge to Terabithia

Disc 2
Track #72

Arranged by
M. C.

Syncopation

Syncopation means placing the accent on a beat (or a part of the beat) which is normally weak. Syncopation is often done by playing a note on the up beat (second half of the beat, or the "*and*") and letting that note ring through the first half of the next beat. Syncopated rhythms are commonly written as a quarter note or quarter notes between two eighth notes. Sometimes the second eighth note is replaced by a dot after the quarter note. The following illustrations show how syncopated rhythms are written out and how they are counted. Some of the songs, exercises, and solos in this book contain these rhythms. It's important that you understand how they are counted. Hold any note and practice tapping your foot on the beat while you play and count the rhythms written below.

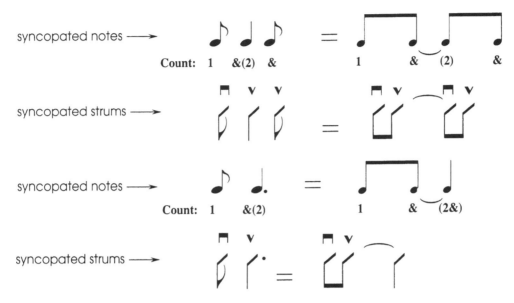

Syncopated Strum Patterns

Shown below are common strum patterns for 4/4 and 3/4 which contain syncopation. They can be used to play the chords to any song in 4/4 or 3/4. Each pattern takes one measure to complete. Hold any chord and practice each pattern. Count aloud as you play the patterns. Be sure to wait for the tied strums.

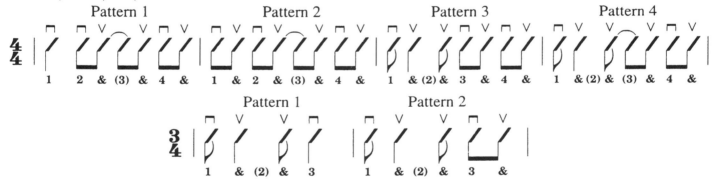

Practice the following exercises which contain **syncopated strums.** Use the pattern which is written in the first measure to play each measure of the exercise.

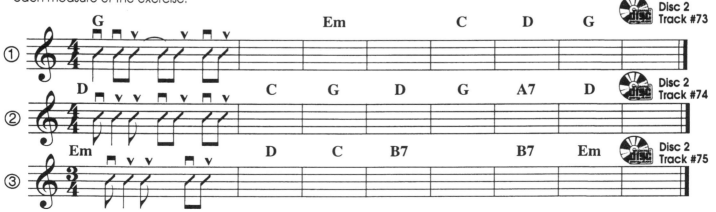

Practice the following song which uses a syncopated strum.

Oh, Sinner Man

Disc 2
Track #76

Oh, sin - ner man ____ where you gon-na run to; Oh, sin - ner

man ____ where you gon - na run to? Oh, sin - ner man ____

where you gon-na run to all ____ on that day? ____

True or False Questions
(Circle the Correct Answer)

1. A sharp raises a note one fret.   True   False

2. Flats lower notes two frets.   True   False

3. Natural signs are placed after notes.   True   False

4. C Sharp and D Flat are located on the same fret.   True   False

5. E Flat and F Natural sound the same.   True   False

Minor Pentatonic Improvisation

When improvising, melodies are created instantly. Rather than simply showing which scale to use and saying "go for it," some guidelines and hints will be helpful in showing how to construct an improvised solo. The material in this section will provide the tools necessary to give "training wheels" for improvisation. Suggestions for which notes, rhythms, and melodic ideas to use will be presented. Build original solos using the suggestions as a starting point. After catching on to the ideas, don't be afraid to experiment.

The scale used in the following exercises is the E minor pentatonic scale. This scale has been presented earlier, but for review, is drawn below. Practice the fingering.

E Minor Pentatonic

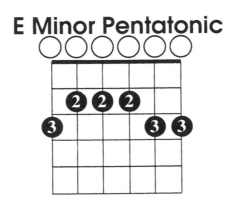

The improvised solos will be played over the chords to the 12-bar blues progression in the key of E. This progression is written below. Become familiar with these chord changes and the sound of the progression.

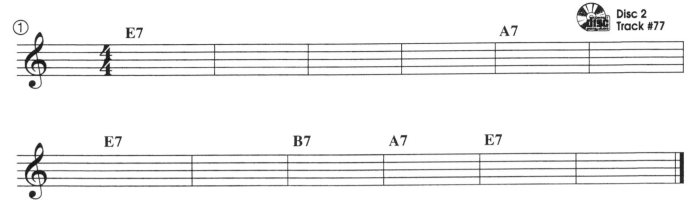

A concern of many guitarists learning to improvise is what rhythms to play. The following exercise will provide a ™rhythm guide.∫ In the exercise below, a part of the solo has been written in every other measure. First practice the exercise playing only the notes which are written and counting (not playing) in the blank measures. Then, play the notes which are written. In the blank measures, play any of the notes from the E minor pentatonic scale (any you would like) using the same rhythm which is written in the previous measure. When improvising to the 12-bar blues progression, any note from the minor pentatonic scale, which has the same letter name as the key, can be used. For example, when improvising to the blues in the key of E, any note from the E minor pentatonic scale can be used. Even when the chords change in the progression (A7 and B7 in blues in E), the notes from the E minor pentatonic scale can be used. Any of the notes from the scale will work, but some will sound better than others. This will be discussed later.

The solo will sound better if large skips are avoided. Play the exercise many times. Each time the exercise is played, use different notes in the blank measures. At first, it may be helpful to write the improvised notes in the blank measures. Then, fill in the blank measures with notes from the E minor pentatonic scale without writing them.

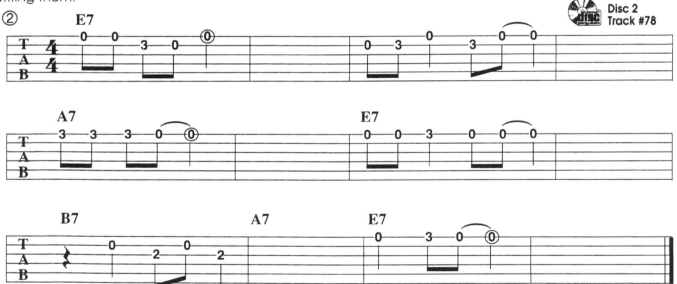

Another improvising concern is which notes to use and in what order the notes of the scale can be played. Remember, when improvising over the 12-bar blues progression, any note from the E minor pentatonic scale can be used in the solo. The next exercise will present some ideas about what order to play the notes from the scale.

In this exercise, play the notes which are written; and in the blank measures, use the same notes which were written in the previous measure, but change the rhythm. Make sure there are four beats in each measure. The rhythms used in the blank measures are up to you, but the notes must be the same as in the previous measure.

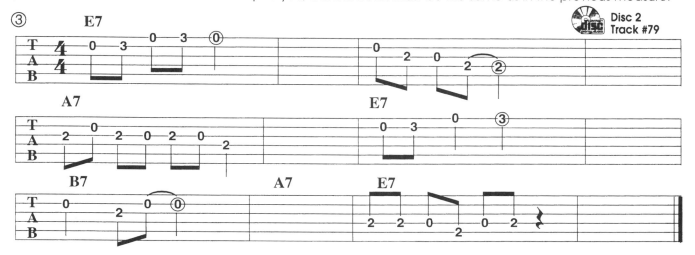

As was mentioned earlier in this section, some notes of the scale will sound better against certain chords. Generally, the notes which will sound the best are chord tones. A chord tone is a note which is contained in the chord being played for a particular measure. The guitar is a great instrument for finding chord tones. Without getting into a lengthy discussion on how chords are constructed, a simple way to find some chord tones is to look at the fingering of the chord. On the three diagrams below, the E minor pentatonic scale has been drawn using circles. The dots show the notes contained in the chord written above the diagram. Some of the notes in the chords will be in the fingering for the E minor pentatonic scale, and others may not. The fingerings for the chords may look a bit different (two notes on the same string). This is because there may be two fingerings for that chord in the first three frets, These are the notes from the scale which will sound the best when playing a solo over that particular chord. One of the best places in the measure to play a chord tone is on the first beat. The other beats can also be chord tones or other notes from the scale.

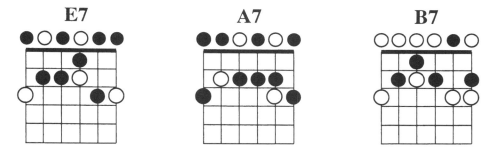

The following exercises will help in learning to use chord tones in building a solo. In the first exercise below, only one chord tone is played in a measure. Notice the note in the measure is a chord tone from the chord for that measure. After playing the exercise as written, play your own "one note solo" using different chord tones.

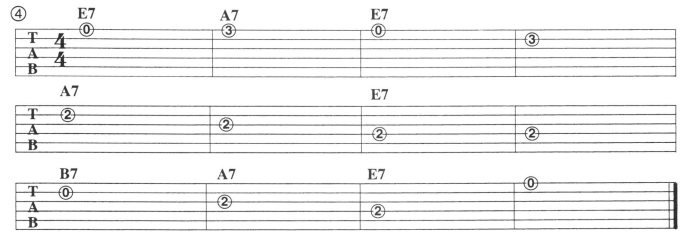

Johann Pachelbel

Johann Pachelbel was a German composer and organist. He was born in 1653 and died in 1706. He was known primarily as a composer of organ and keyboard music, although he did write a large number of sacred choral works. The Canon is his most famous composition. A canon is a musical form popularized during the Renaissance which is similar to a round. With a canon, each part duplicates the melody played previously.

Pachelbel's Canon

Disc 2
Track #80

Arranged by
M. C.

The "F" Chord
(Student plays the top 4 strings)

Disc 2
Track #81

To play the F chord - make sure your left hand thumb is on the center of the back of the neck. If you wrap your thumb around the neck so that it touches the 6th string, you will have problems fingering the F chord.

Building the F Chord

Play the following exercise until the tone sounds clear. Start on the 1st fret and end on the 7th fret.

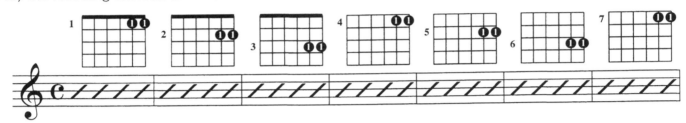

Now play this exercise from the 1st to the 7th fret until it sounds clear.

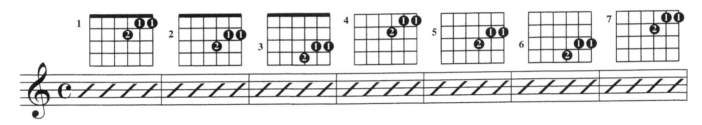

Play from the 1st to the 7th fret until it sounds clear.

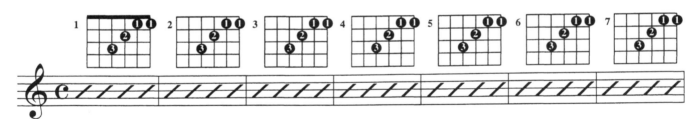

New Chords

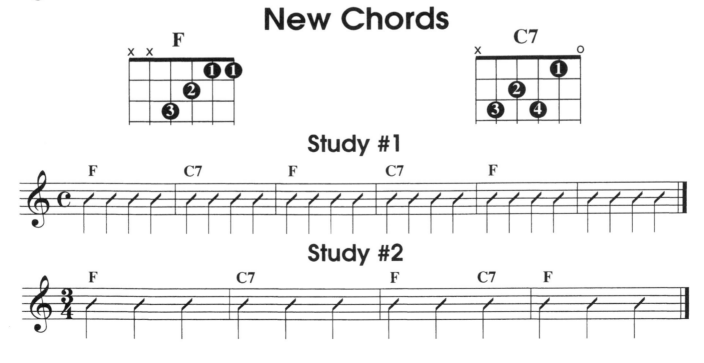

Study #1

Study #2

La Cucaracha

Allegro
Strum
Disc 2 Track #82
MEXICAN

Cuan-do u-no quie re u - na___ Y_es-ta u-na no lo quie - re,___

Es lo mis-mo que si_un cal - vo,___ En la ca_lle en-cuen-tra_un pei - ne.___ La Cu-ca-

ra - cha,___ la Cu-ca - ra - cha,___ Ya no quiere ca - mi - nar,___ Por que no

tie - ne,___ por-que le fal - ta___ la pa-ti - ca prin-ci - pal.

Comin' Through the Rye

Andante
Strum
Disc 2 Track #83
SCOTTISH BALLAD

If a bod-y meets a bod-y com-in' through the rye.

If a bod-y kiss a bod-y, need a bod-y cry?

Ev - ry las-sie has a lad-die, none, they say, have I, yet

all the lads, they smile on me when com-in' through the rye.

Alternating Bass

A type of accompaniment which is very popular on the guitar is alternating bass. This style of accompaniment is also referred to as alternating pick-strum, western swing, or Carter style. Alternating bass can be simple to learn and provides a great accompaniment for singers.

To learn this style, divide the chords you have learned into the following three categories: 1) 6-string chords (chords on which 6 strings are strummed, like G and Em) 2) 5-string chords (chords on which 5 strings are strummed, like C and Am) and 3) 4-string chords (chords where 4 strings are strummed, like D and F).

The first alternating bass pattern we will play works for 4/4 time. The pattern takes one measure to complete. For one measure of a 6-string chord (such as G), the pattern is written below.

The numbers show the individual strings to pick. The picking of a single string is followed by a strum. The strums are down strums. Pick the sixth string, then strum the chord. This is followed by picking the fifth string and strumming the chord. The stems under the numbers are like the stems on quarter notes. They show that picking the string takes one beat. The single strings are picked with the right-hand thumb and the strum is done with right-hand first, second and third fingers. The strum is done by starting with the fingers curled and while strumming across the strings, straightening them. The alternating bass may also be done with a pick. Be sure to pick and strum the strings straight down. After picking the sixth string, either five or six strings may be strummed.

Practice doing the alternating bass pattern for 4/4 in the following progression.

Disc 2
Track #84

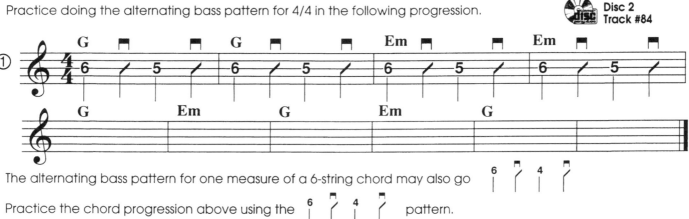

The alternating bass pattern for one measure of a 6-string chord may also go

Practice the chord progression above using the pattern.

The pattern for one measure of a 5-string chord (like C) is written below. This can be done with the thumb and fingers or a pick. After picking the fifth string, four strings may be strummed or the fifth string can also be included in the strum.

Practice the following progression using the fifth string alternating bass.

Disc 2
Track #85

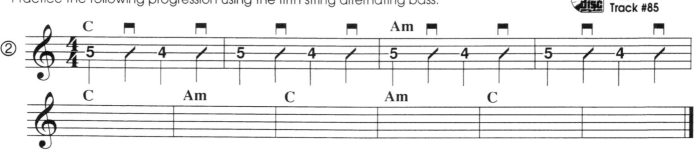

The 4/4 alternating bass pattern for one measure of a four-string chord is written below.

Practice the following chords using the alternating bass for 4-string chords. When playing the F chord, it will sound better for now to play   rather than

Practice the following chord progression using alternating bass patterns for 6-string, 5-string, and 4-string chords. The patterns are written in the measures on the first line. Depending on whether the chord is a 6-, 5-, or 4-string chord, play the appropriate patterns on the second and third lines.

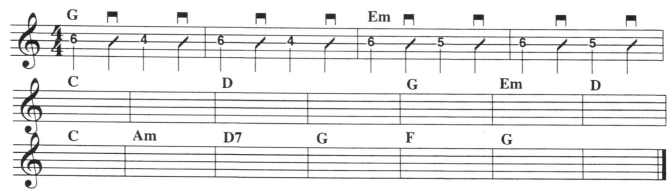

The alternating bass style of accompaniment can be used to play many songs in 4/4. Play the following songs using alternating bass. The patterns are written above the first few measures. Remember the patterns take one measure to complete. After playing those songs, go back and play earlier songs from this book in 4/4 which were strummed, only now use the alternating bass.

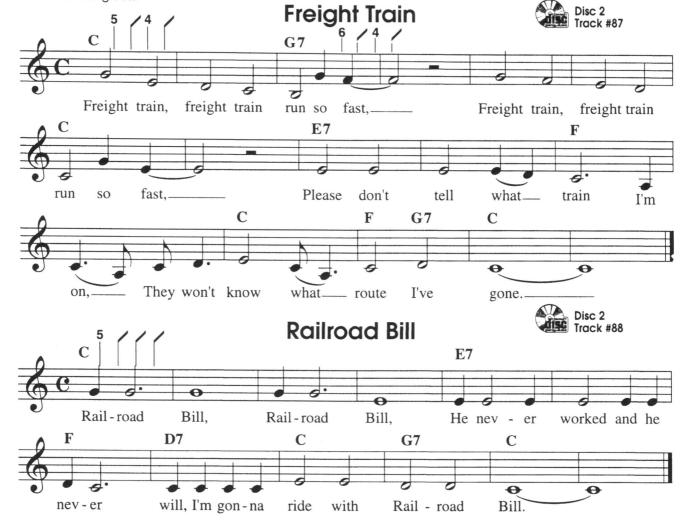

Freight Train

Railroad Bill

Nine Pound Hammer

Railroad Song

Disc 2
Track #89

This nine-pound ham-mer   is a lit-tle too heav-y

Bud-dy for my size.   Bud-dy for my size.

CHORUS

So roll on bud-dy   Don't you roll so slow,

How can I roll   When the wheels won't go?

So roll on bud-dy,   pull a load of coal.

How can I pull   When the wheels won't roll?

2. I'm going to the mountain
   For to see my darlin'
   But I ain't coming back
   No I ain't coming back. *Chorus*

3. Ain't one hammer
   In this whole tunnel
   That rings like mine
   That rings like mine. *Chorus*

4. Rings like silver
   Shines like gold
   Oh it rings like silver
   And it shines like gold. *Chorus*

 Disc 2
Track #90

Alternating Bass For 3/4 Time

The 3/4 alternating bass patterns are written below. Each pattern takes one measure of 3/4 to complete. Notice that the lowest note in the chord is picked, followed by two strums.

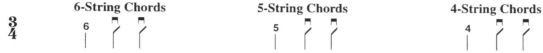

Practice the following progression using the alternating bass for 3/4. The patterns have been written in the first 16 measures. After that, choose and play the correct pattern depending on whether the chord for that measure is a 6-, 5-, or 4-string chord.

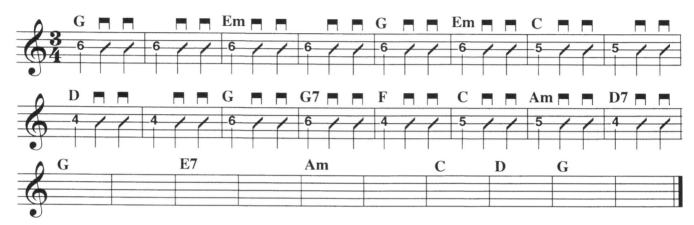

Practice the following song using alternating bass for 3/4 time. The patterns have been written above the first measure of each new chord.

Silent Night

Franz Grüber

Disc 2
Track #91

2. Silent night, holy night,
Shepherds quake at the sight,
Glories stream from heaven afar,
Heavenly hosts sing Alleluia;
Christ the Savior is born!
Christ the Savior is born!

3. Silent, night, holy night,
Son of God, love's pure light
Radiant beams from Thy holy face,
With the dawn of redeeming grace,
Jesus, Lord, at Thy birth,
Jesus, Lord, at Thy birth.

4. Silent night, holy night,
Wondrous Star, lend thy light;
With the angels let us sing,
Alleluia to our King;
Christ the Savior is born,
Christ the Savior is born.

Acres of Bluegrass
(For Two or Three Guitars)

Disc 2
Track #92

Guitar III should play the chords using the alternating pick-strum accompaniment such as the pattern written above measure six.

Arranged by
M. C.

Outsiders' Blues
Guitar Ensemble

Disc 2
Track #93

Arranged by
M. C.

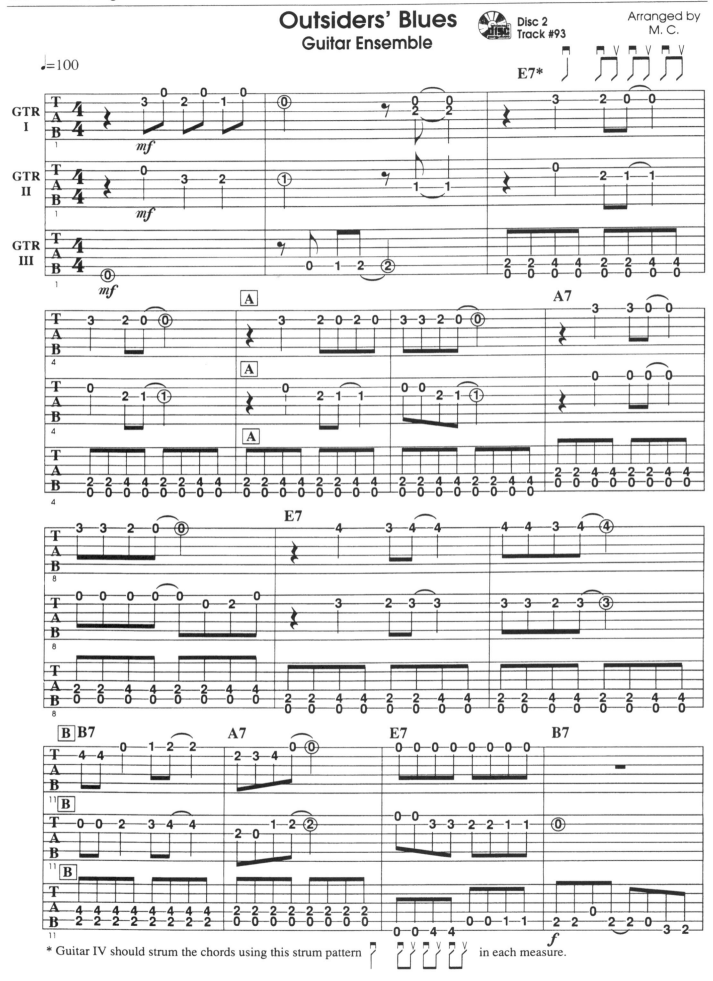

* Guitar IV should strum the chords using this strum pattern in each measure.

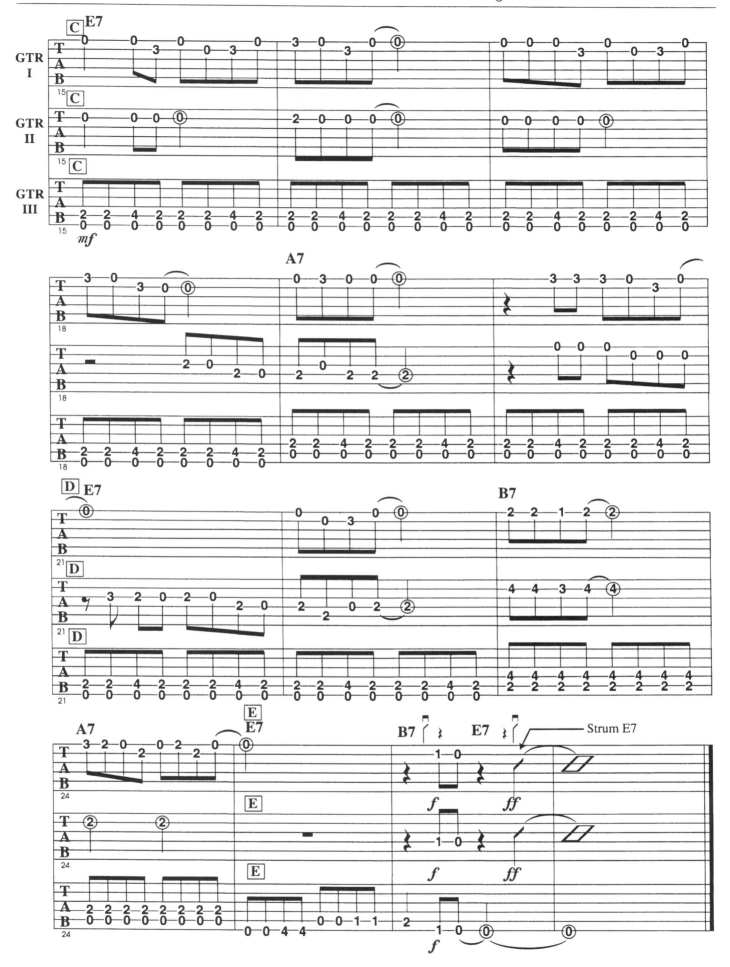

Notation Guide

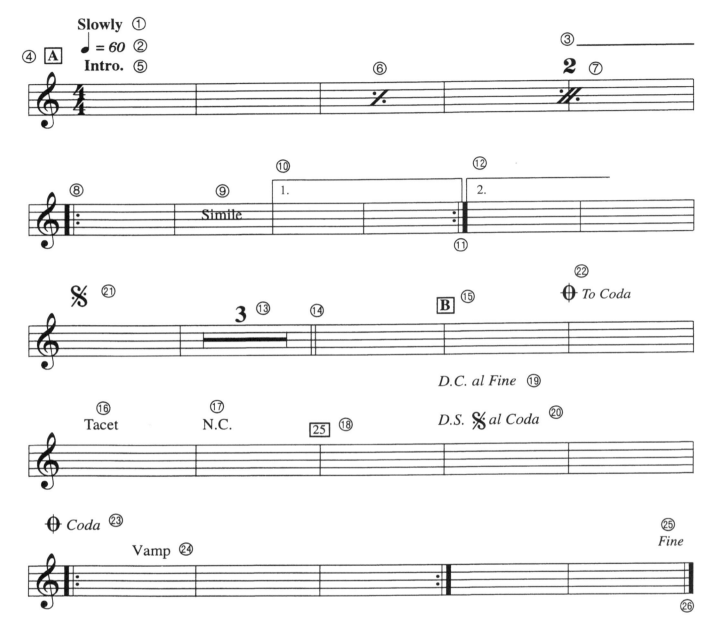

Notation Guide

① **Style Description.** Indicates the style and possibly the tempo of the music.

② **Tempo Indication.** Indicates the tempo of the music by showing the number of beats per minute.

③ **Composer.** The composer's name goes here.

④ **Rehearsal Cue.** Indicates a particular section of the music. These cues are often used in rehearsal to locate beginning points (can be numbers rather than letters).

⑤ **Introduction.** Indicates this section is the introduction of the piece.

⑥ **Repeat.** Repeat the previous measure.

⑦ **Repeat.** Repeat the previous two measures.

⑧ **Repeat sign.** After playing to the repeat sign with the two dots on the left (no. 11), repeat to this spot.

⑨ **Simile.** In this measure, play what was written in the previous measure (in a similar manner).

⑩ **First Ending.** The first time through play this portion of the music.

⑪ **Repeat sign.** Repeat from this point to the repeat sign written earlier which has the two dots on the right of the double line.

⑫ **Second ending.** After repeating, skip the first ending and go to the second ending.

⑬ **Rest.** Rest for the number of measures indicated.

⑭ **End of Section.** Two thin double lines indicate the end of a section of music (i.e. the chorus).

⑮ **Rehearsal Cue.** Indicates the beginning of the B section in the music.

⑯ **Tacet.** Indicates the accompaniment is to stop.

⑰ **N.C. Indicates** "No Chord." The chord (the accompaniment) stops for this portion of the music.

⑱ **Rehearsal Cue.** Indicates a particular measure number in the music (in this case, measure 25).

⑲ **D.C. al Fine.** D.C. (da capo) means to repeat the beginning of the piece. "al Fine" means play to the point where "Fine" is written.

⑳ **D.S. 𝄋 al Fine.** D.S. 𝄋 (da signo) indicates to repeat from this point to the D.S. sign, "al coda" means to play to the point where "to Coda" is written.

㉑ **D.S. Sign. (𝄋)** After playing to the point where D.S. 𝄋 is written, repeat to the place where this sign 𝄋 is written.

㉒ **To Coda.** After doing all of the repeats, go from ⊕ to Coda to the place near the end of the piece where ⊕ Coda is written.

㉓ **Coda (⊕).** The ending of the music.

㉔ **Vamp.** Repeat this portion of the music as many times as desired, or until directed to continue.

㉕ **Fine.** Means "finish" or end the music here.

㉖ **Thin/Heavy Double Line.** Indicates the end of the piece.

Tempo

Largo. Very slow.

Adagio. Slowly.

Andante. Walking speed.

Moderato. Moderately, medium speed.

Allegro. Quickly, fast.

Rubato. No set tempo, notes may be held longer or shorter than their exact value.

rit. Ritardando, gradually get slower.

Dynamics

pp **(pianissimo).** Very soft.

p **(piano).** Soft.

mp **(mezzo piano).** Medium soft.

mf **(mezzo forte).** Medium loud.

f **(forte).** Loud.

ff **(fortissimo).** Very loud.

> (crescendo). Gradually get louder.

< (de crescendo). Gradually get softer.

> (accent). The note is to be played louder.

Reference Chord Chart

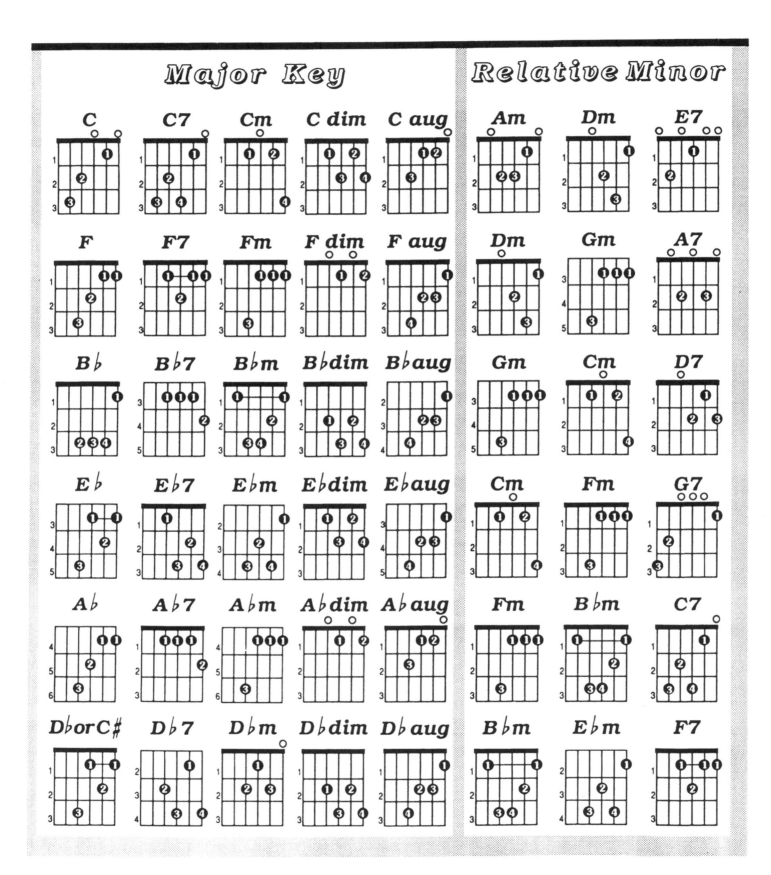

Reference Chord Chart

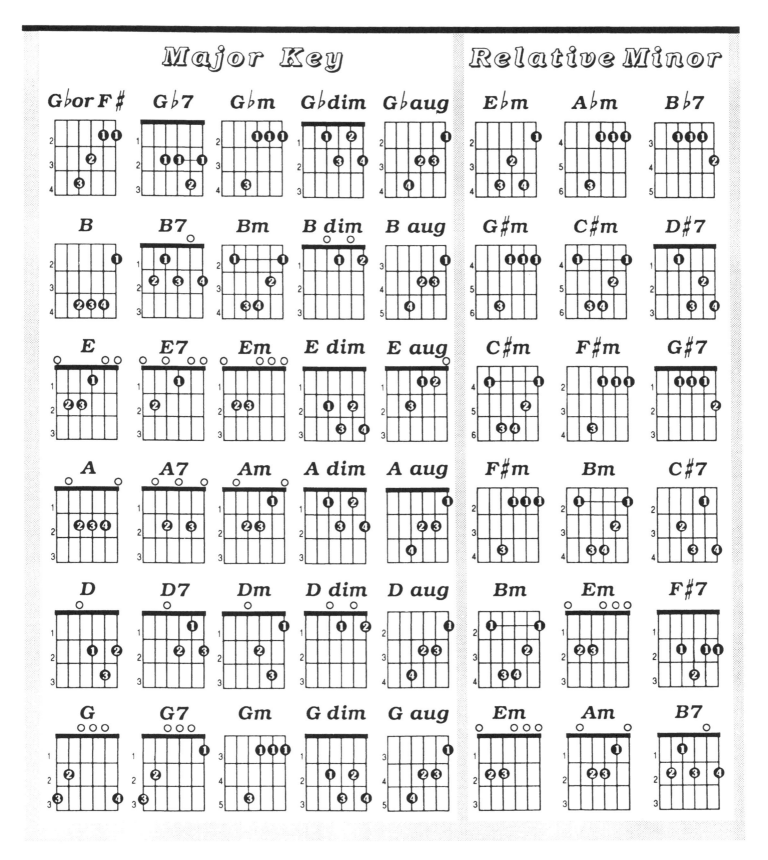

Notes/Manuscript

Notes/Tab

Notes/Chord Diagram

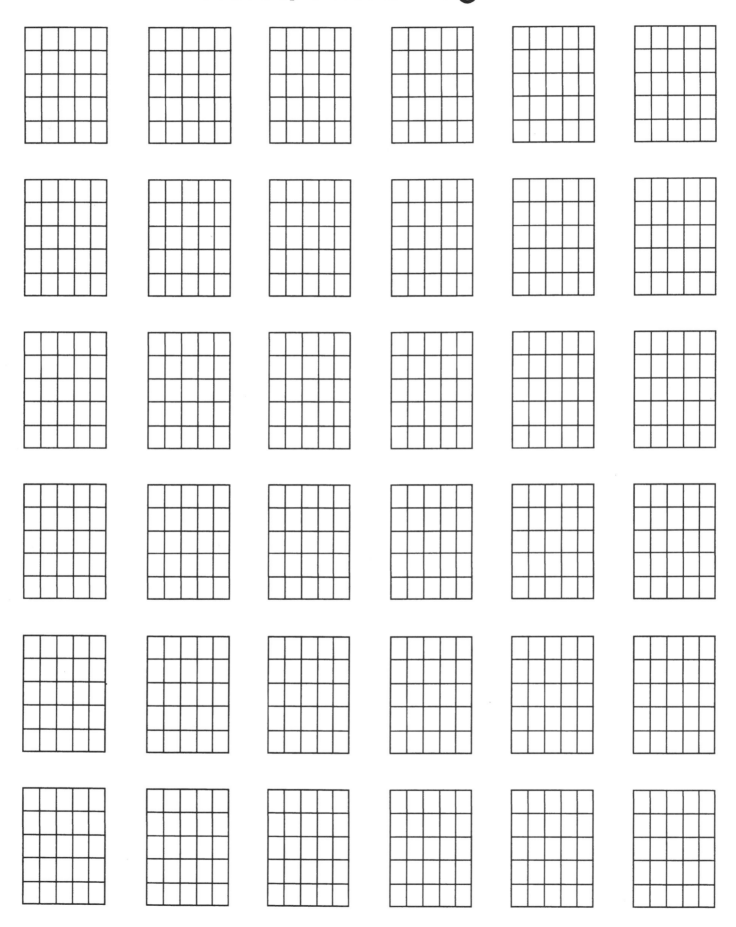